# POST CORONA

# POST CORONA

## FROM CRISIS
## TO OPPORTUNITY

## Scott Galloway

PORTFOLIO | PENGUIN

PORTFOLIO / PENGUIN
An imprint of Penguin Random House LLC
penguinrandomhouse.com

Most Portfolio books are available at a discount when purchased in quantity for sales
promotions or corporate use. Special editions, which include personalized covers, excerpts,
and corporate imprints, can be created when purchased in large quantities. For more
information, please call (212) 572-2232 or e-mail specialmarkets@penguinrandomhouse.com.
Your local bookstore can also assist with discounted bulk purchases using the Penguin
Random House corporate Business-to-Business program. For assistance in locating a
participating retailer, e-mail B2B@penguinrandomhouse.com.

Illustrations copyright © 2020 by Section4

Library of Congress Control Number: 2020946847

ISBN 9780593332214 (hardcover)
ISBN 9780593332221 (ebook)

Printed in the United States of America
1   3   5   7   9   10   8   6   4   2

BOOK DESIGN BY MEIGHAN CAVANAUGH

*For California taxpayers and the*
*Regents of the University of California*

# CONTENTS

# INTRODUCTION

We're taught time is a reliable, relentless force. The sun's progress across the sky and our seasonal orbit around the sun establish an immortal, uniform rhythm. However, our perception of time is not constant. As we age, our frame of reference (the past) expands, and the years move faster. This morning I kissed my son goodbye before his first day of kindergarten. This afternoon he came home from fifth grade. It's the opposite for him. His school believes that same fifth grade should be a safe place to fail. His first Cs and Ds arrest time, frequently.

What we experience is change, not time. Aristotle observed that time does not exist without change, because what we call time is simply our measurement of the difference between "before" and "after."[1] Hence our daily experience of time dragging or flying by. Time is malleable, paced by change. And the smallest thing can create unprecedented change. Even something as small as a virus.

In early March of 2020, we were living in the "before." The novel coronavirus was in the news, but just. Outside China there was little to suggest a global crisis was unfolding. Forty-one people had died in northern Italy, but in the rest of Europe life was unchanged. The United States reported its first death on March 1, but the big news was Mayor Pete suspended his campaign for the presidency. There were no closures, no masks, and most people wouldn't have recognized Dr. Anthony Fauci.

By the end of the month, we were in the "after." The world shut down. Hundreds of thousands of people tested positive for the virus, including Tom Hanks, Placido Domingo, Boris Johnson, and dozens of sailors on a U.S. aircraft carrier in the middle of the Pacific Ocean.

A virus one four-hundredth the width of a human hair grabbed a sphere weighing 13 billion trillion tons and set it spinning ten times faster.

Yet even as time (change) sped up, our lives felt static. Like my son holding his first bad report card, we lost our capacity to imagine anything beyond the present moment. No before *or* after, just Zoom calls, takeout, and Netflix. We checked case counts and deaths vs. game scores and movie times. The hit movie of summer was *Palm Springs*—a story of two people living the same day over and over again.

Having experienced fifty-odd trips around the sun, I know

we are wrong about the persistence of this moment. I try to convince myself what I tell my boys: this too shall pass. This book is an attempt to look beyond our unprecedented present and predict the future by creating it, catalyzing a dialog that crafts better solutions.

When the only astronomical object known to harbor life reverts to its regular rate of rotation, what will be different about business, education, and our country? Will it be more humane and prosperous? Or will people prefer it just stop spinning? What can we do to shape the "after"?

I'm an entrepreneur and a business school professor, so I view things through the lens of business. That's the core of this book—how the pandemic will reshape the business environment. I examine how the pandemic has favored big companies, and big tech most of all. A healthy portion of this book is a pandemic-era update to my first book, *The Four*, revisiting Amazon, Apple, Facebook, and Google. I also look at the disruption opportunities outside the sectors dominated by the Four, and some of the firms poised to prosper.

Business doesn't operate in a vacuum, so I connect the business story to our broader societal story. I've devoted an entire chapter to higher education, as I believe it is on the cusp of transformative change. I write about the ways in which the pandemic has revealed and accelerated broader trends in our culture and politics, why I believe that a generation of changes undertaken in the name of capitalism have undermined the capitalist system, and what we can do about it. This has been a worldwide crisis, and while my examples and analysis are rooted in a U.S. experience, I hope these insights will hold value for readers in other countries.

I begin with two theses. **First, the pandemic's most enduring impact will be as an accelerant.** While it will initiate some changes and alter the direction of some trends, the pandemic's primary effect has been to accelerate dynamics already present in society. **Second, in any crisis there is opportunity; the greater and more disruptive the crisis, the greater the opportunities.** However, my optimism on the second point is tempered by the first—many of the trends the pandemic accelerates are negative and weaken our capacity to recover and thrive in a post-corona world.

## The Great Acceleration

There is a saying attributed to Lenin: **"Nothing can happen for decades, and then decades can happen in weeks."** It wasn't Lenin, but Scottish MP George Galloway (great name). Galloway was paraphrasing, with typical Scottish brevity, something much more roundabout and obtuse that Lenin said in 1918, after the radical changes wrought by his revolution.

This theme, decades in weeks, is playing out in most sectors and facets of life. Ecommerce began taking root in 2000. Since then, ecommerce's share of retail has grown approximately 1% every year. At the beginning of 2020, approximately 16% of retail was transacted via digital channels. Eight weeks after the pandemic reached the U.S. (March to mid-April), that number leapt to 27% . . . and it's not going back. We registered a decade of ecommerce growth in eight weeks.

## U.S. ECOMMERCE PENETRATION
### (% OF RETAIL SALES)
2009–2020

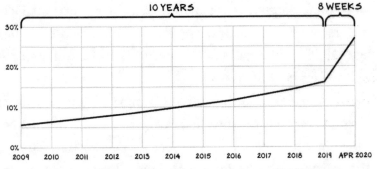

SOURCE: BANK OF AMERICA, U.S. DEPARTMENT OF COMMERCE, SHAWSPRING RESEARCH.

Take any trend—social, business, or personal—and fast-forward ten years. Even if your firm isn't there yet, consumer behavior and the market now rests on the 2030 point on the trend line—positive or negative. If your firm had a weak balance sheet, it's now untenable. If you're in essential retail, your goods are more essential than ever. If you're in discretionary retail, you are more discretionary than ever. In your personal life, if you were fighting with your partner, your rows are worse. Good relationships now have another ten years of history and goodwill.

For decades, companies invested millions of dollars in equipment for virtual meetings, hoping to diminish distance. Universities begrudgingly adopted tech tools including Blackboard in the early '90s to (sort of) keep pace with the outside world. Communications companies ran numerous ads featuring virtual family dinners, doctors seeing patients from across the country, and students learning from the world's great teachers without leaving their hometown.

And for decades, not much happened. Multimillion-dollar video conference systems didn't work, and faculty resisted any tech more complex than Dry Erase or PowerPoint. FaceTime and Skype made inroads in our personal communications, but didn't reach critical mass.

Then, in weeks, our lives moved online and business went remote. Every business meeting went virtual, every teacher became an online educator, and social gatherings moved to a screen. In the markets, investors calibrated the value of disruptive companies based not on the next weeks or years, but on assumptions of the firm's position in 2030.

It took Apple 42 years to reach $1 trillion in value, and 20 weeks to accelerate from $1 trillion to $2 trillion (March to August 2020). In those same weeks, Tesla became not only the most valuable car company in the world, but more valuable than Toyota, Volkswagen, Daimler, and Honda . . . combined.

For decades, big-city mayors and planning officials have been calling for more bike lanes, pedestrian access, and fewer cars. And for decades, traffic, air pollution, and accidents congested our streets and skies. Then, in weeks, cyclists took over the road, outdoor dining tables sprouted, and skies cleared.

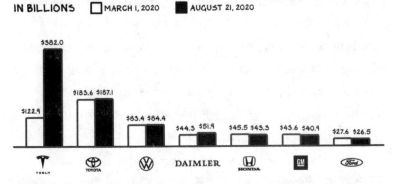

## MARKET CAPITALIZATION OF AUTO FIRMS

IN BILLIONS ☐ MARCH 1, 2020 ■ AUGUST 21, 2020

SOURCE: ANALYSIS OF SEEKING ALPHA DATA.

Negative trends may have accelerated at a greater rate. For decades, economists have been warning that economic inequality was deepening, while economic mobility was declining. An economy with uncomfortable underlying trends has morphed to a dystopia.

Forty percent of Americans, we were told, would have trouble covering a $400 emergency expense. But an unprecedented 11-year economic expansion meant the tide never went out. Then, in the first three months of the Covid-19 recession we lost more employment (13%) than we lost in the two years of the Great Recession (5%). Half of U.S. households have had at least one person lose a job or take a pay cut because of the outbreak.[2] Households with income below $40,000 were hit hardest—almost 40% were laid off or furloughed by early April, compared to just 13% of households with income over $100,000.[3]

The world spun faster, for better or worse.

# In Crisis There Is Opportunity

It's a cliché for a reason. John F. Kennedy made it a staple of his campaign speeches. Al Gore used it in his Nobel Prize acceptance speech. The Chinese word for *crisis* consists of two symbols, one meaning *danger,* the other, we are told, meaning *opportunity.* What opportunities await us post corona?

The pandemic has a silver lining that could rival the size of the cloud. America overnight has a greater savings rate and fewer emissions. Three of the largest, and most important, consumer categories in the U.S. (healthcare, education, and grocery) are in a state of unprecedented disruption and, possibly, progress.

While the overwhelming of some hospitals due to Covid-19 was rightfully the lead story, the more lasting narrative may be how the other 99% of people accessed healthcare during the pandemic—without setting foot in a doctor's office, much less a hospital. The forced embrace of telemedicine promises an explosion in innovation and opens a new front in the war against the costs and burdens of our broken healthcare system. Similarly, the forced embrace of remote learning, as clunky and problematic as it has been, could catalyze the evolution of higher education, yielding lower costs and increased admittance rates, and restoring college to its role as the lubricant for Americans' upward mobility. Even more fundamental than education, nutrition stands on the precipice of revolution, if the dispersion of grocery via delivery creates opportunities for more efficient distribution, wider reach for fresh foods, and adoption of local goods.

Underneath these changes, coming of age in a worldwide crisis has the potential to mature a generation with a renewed appreciation for community, cooperation, and sacrifice—a generation that believes empathy is not weakness, and wealth isn't virtue.

Opportunities are not guarantees. Indeed, the popular story about the Chinese word for *crisis* is not quite right. The first character means *danger*, but the second character is better translated as *a critical juncture*. A crossroads. For Lenin's countrymen, the radical transformations of 1917 presented opportunities as well. Their failure to seize them led to immense suffering.

It's easy to believe that won't happen to us, that "it can't happen here." But consider that not long ago (middle of the 20th century), we put 75,000 American citizens behind barbed wire because they had Japanese ancestry. Consider that none of us, at the onset of the pandemic, thought the U.S. could be a country that lost a thousand people a day to a virus that other (less developed?) nations stopped in its tracks.

Our response to this crisis has not inspired confidence. Despite having longer to prepare, spending more on healthcare than any nation, and believing we are the most innovative society in history, with 5% of the world's population the U.S. has endured 25% of the infections and deaths. It took the last

10 years to create 20 million jobs and 10 weeks to destroy 40 million. Travel is down, restaurants are dark, drinking and handgun sales are up. Over 2 million Gen Zers have moved back in with their parents,[4] and 75 million young people are going to school amidst uncertainty, conflict, and danger.

## CHANGE IN BEHAVIOR
## PRE AND POST PANDEMIC
### APRIL 2019 VS. APRIL 2020

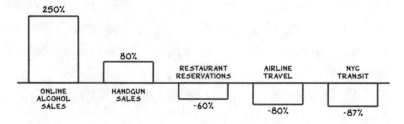

SOURCES: I. NOWTHISNEWS 2. NPR 3. CNN 4. CNBC 5. NYT.

Historians can dissect the missteps that led us here. The deeper cause of our failure is already clear.

Consider two wars. America's involvement in World War II lasted 3 years and 8 months, and 407,000 Americans perished. You couldn't find chocolate or nylons, and despite the financial stress of wartime, households were asked to dig into their pockets and buy war bonds. Manufacturers retooled their plants to build bombers and tanks, and a nationwide 35 miles per hour "Victory" speed limit was imposed to save fuel and rubber for the war effort.[5] We drafted high school students and high school teachers, and they gave their lives for liberty. After the war, we invested in our enemies and produced more wealth and prosperity than any society to date. For a time, we distributed it more fairly than ever before. We changed where we lived (suburbs) and how we lived (the car and television), and began a long-overdue reckoning with our most profound inequalities of race and gender.

## OUTSOURCING SACRIFICE

American forces have been fighting in Afghanistan for 19 years, and we've lost 2,312 service members. The conflict has metastasized into violence spanning half the globe, with civilian deaths in the untold (literally) hundreds of thousands. During that time, I have seen numerous 14-mile-per-gallon SUVs with "Support Our Troops" bumper stickers, but I've had no trouble finding chocolate, or anything else I might desire, at the store or on my phone. The more money I make, the lower my tax rate, and nobody has asked me to buy a war bond or take a draft number. Instead, we have outsourced the war to a volunteer army of working-class young people, financed by future generations via a $6.5 trillion increase in the deficit.[6]

Patriotism used to be sacrifice, now it's stimulus. In the pandemic, our nation and its leaders have spoken with their actions: millions of American deaths would be bad, but a decline in the NASDAQ would be tragic. The result has been disproportionate suffering. Lower-income Americans and people of color are more likely to be infected and face twice the risk of serious illness than people from higher-income households.[7] For the wealthy, time with family, Netflix, savings, and stock portfolio value have all increased as commutes and costs have declined.

Whether the U.S. is headed for a Hunger Games future or something brighter depends on which path we choose post corona.

# [ 1 ]

# COVID & THE CULLING

## The Culling of the Herd:
## The Strong Get (Much) Stronger

One of the most surprising aspects of the Covid crisis has been the resilience of the capital markets. After a brief plunge when the outbreak graduated to pandemic, the major market indexes (Dow Jones, S&P 500, NASDAQ Composite) roared back. By summer, they had regained most of the lost ground, despite over 180,000 U.S. deaths, record unemployment, and no sign of the virus receding. *Bloomberg Businessweek* called it "The Great Disconnect" in a June cover story.[1] Even the "Wall Street pros," the magazine declared, were "flabbergasted." Two months later, at the time of this writing, the virus is killing a thousand Americans per day, and market indexes continue to climb.

Market indexes can be misleading, however. The "recovery" has been the product of outsized gains by a few firms, notably the big tech companies and other major players. It's not reflected in the broader public markets. From January 1 through July 31, 2020, the S&P 500, which tracks the 500 largest public companies, was just positive on the year. But companies in the middle, mid-caps, were down 10%. And the 600 small-cap companies tracked in the S&P 600 were off 15%.

## STOCK PERFORMANCE OF S&P SMALL CAP, MID CAP, AND LARGE CAP INDICES
JANUARY 1 — JULY 31, 2020

SOURCE: ANALYSIS OF YAHOO FINANCE DATA.

While the media has been distracted by shiny objects like big tech and large-cap indexes, a relentless culling of the herd is well underway. The weak are not merely falling behind, they are being slaughtered. The list of bankruptcies is long and shocking: Neiman Marcus, J.Crew, JCPenney, and Brooks Brothers; Hertz (which owns Dollar and Thrifty) and Advantage; Lord & Taylor, True Religion, Lucky Brand Jeans, Ann Taylor, Lane Bryant, Men's Wearhouse, and John Varvatos; 24 Hour Fitness, Gold's Gym, GNC, Modell's Sporting Goods, and the XFL; Sur la Table, Dean & DeLuca, and Muji; Chesapeake Energy, Diamond Offshore, and Whiting Petroleum; California Pizza Kitchen, the U.S. arm of Le Pain Quotidien, and Chuck E. Cheese.[2] "BEACH" stocks (booking, entertainment, airlines, cruises and casinos, hotels and resorts) are down 50–70% on average.[3]

This helps explain the strong performance of the market leaders. A firm's valuation is a function of its numbers and narrative. Right now, size can feed a narrative not just about how a company will survive the crisis, but how it will thrive in the post-corona world. Post culling, when the rains return, there is more foliage for fewer elephants. Companies with cash, with debt collateral, with highly valued stock will be positioned to acquire the assets of distressed competitors and consolidate the market.

The pandemic is also boosting an "innovation" narrative. Firms deemed innovators are receiving a valuation that reflects estimates of cash flows 10 years from now, and discounted back at an incredibly low rate. Investors appear to be focused on a firm's vision, its narrative about where it could be in a decade. That's how Tesla's value now exceeds that of Toyota, Volkswagen, Daimler, and Honda combined. That's despite the fact that in 2020 Tesla will produce approximately 400,000 vehicles, while the other four companies will build a combined 26,000,000.

The market is making bold bets about the post-corona environment, and we are seeing both big gains and steep declines. At the end of July, Tesla was up 242% on the year, while GM was down 31%. Amazon was up 67%, and JCPenney was bankrupt. This "disconnect"—between the big and the small, the innovative and the old fashioned—is as important as the more talked-about gap between the market and the broader economy. Today's winners are judged tomorrow's bigger winners, and today's losers appear doomed.

## THE STRONG GET STRONGER
**IMPLIED PROFIT BASED ON CHANGES IN MARKET CAPITALIZATION 2002–2020**

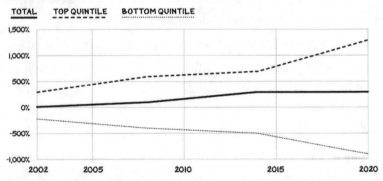

NOTE: LARGEST 2,562 COMPANIES BY REVENUE. SOURCE: MCKINSEY & COMPANY, VARIANCE.

The thing about capital market predictions is that they are to an extent self-fulfilling. By deciding that Amazon, Tesla, and other promising companies are winners, the markets lower those companies' cost of capital, increase the value of their compensation (via stock options), and enhance their ability to acquire what they cannot build themselves. And there is an incredible amount of capital looking for a home right now. The U.S. government has poured $2.2 trillion into the economy, and because of some terrible policy decisions (more on that later) a huge amount of that is going right into the capital markets. So companies that were doing well before the pandemic hit have benefited remarkably from this worldwide crisis. They found funding available to absorb revenue losses, bulk up against the competition, and expand into the new opportunities the pandemic is opening up. Meanwhile, their weaker competitors have been shut out of the capital markets and will see their debt ratings cut, the holders of their payables come calling, and customers skittish about long-term deals.

There is a non-economic arbiter to who perishes, survives, or thrives: government support. Airlines, for example, are in no kind of shape to survive this pandemic in their current form. It's difficult to envision a product more conducive to the spread of a virus than an airplane. The pandemic accelerates remote work and obviates business travel, the industry's cash cow. In addition, airlines have huge overhead and difficulty reducing costs when revenues drop. Several smaller domestic airlines, not seen as national champions, and a number of foreign carriers, including Virgin Atlantic, have declared bankruptcy. But I suspect we won't see a single major U.S. carrier go under, because the airlines have a death grip on the U.S. Congress. In April 2020, the government gave them $25 billion, and they will likely get more. A combination of good lobbyists and PR people, high consumer awareness, and a deep connection to national pride can save an industry by giving it a capital lifeline from history's deepest pocket.

## Surviving the Culling: Cash Is King

For the last decade, the markets have replaced profits with vision and growth when determining the value of a company. Blitzscale, at any cost. Costs are just investment, and profits or dominance will come. Why not? Cash flow is irrelevant when equity investors are lining up to invest more capital, and with a history of taking very little debt and thriving on intangible assets, tech balance sheets in particular received little scrutiny.

In the pandemic, however, cash is king, and cost structure is the new blood oxygen level. Strong balance sheets mean capital to get through the lean times. Companies with cash, low debt or cheap debt, high-value assets, and low fixed costs will likely survive.

Costco is well positioned to buck the ugly trends in retail for a number of reasons, including 11 billion of them sitting in its bank account. Honeywell's $15 billion will likely carry it into a post-corona land of milk and honey. Johnson & Johnson has nearly $20 billion—it's not going anywhere. Every one of these companies will have their pick of the assets and customers left behind when their weaker competitors shut down. In every category, there will be more concentration of power in the two or three companies with the strongest balance sheets.

There's been a lot of talk in the past few years about the problem of share buybacks—companies using earnings to purchase their own shares. That juices the stock price, often leading to large bonuses for senior management, but at no benefit to the underlying businesses. As we crash into a recession, management is going to have second thoughts about this strategy. They are going to want that cash back, but it's too late. Share buybacks have always been ticking time bombs, trading the long-term future of the company for short-term investment returns, and now those bombs are detonating. These firms should be allowed to fail. Not to let them fail is to decide, as an economy, that we favor equity over debt, as the debt holders should own these assets.

The biggest toll will be on bigger companies with a lot of employees that had a bad balance sheet. I said in March 2020[4] that Ann Taylor will go away, and by July its operator, Ascena, filed for bankruptcy, owing $10–$50 billion to 100,000 lenders, mostly real estate owners. Chico's will also go away. Failure to innovate and attract a younger, more online customer base has been lethal to traditional retail even pre Covid. Medium and large companies with weak balance sheets will create the most damage from an economic standpoint. This is the challenge with owning a restaurant. A large fixed cost—your lease—and little or nothing you can do about it, and because it's a low-margin business with few sources of funding, there's typically no capital cushion to survive lean times.

## Crisis Management 101

At the outset of addressing this crisis, it's essential to understand where a company is on the strategic spectrum of the pandemic. The right moves for the biggest elephant in the herd are not the smart play for a "sickly gazelle" (how Jeff Bezos once described small book publishers). Sector plays a big role here: some are doing great (technology), some are just okay (transportation, healthcare), and some are struggling (restaurants, hospitality). Within sectors, relative strength in key metrics (brand, management, balance sheet) call for different strategies. Even in the weakest sector, someone will come through the other side.

But many won't. Stubbornness is a virtue to a point, but companies in hard-hit sectors that are not in a position to feast on weaker competitors need to think well outside the box. Is there a pivot available? An asset that can be bridged to a new business? For example, I'm an investor and on the board of the nation's largest yellow pages company. Now, they are morphing into a customer relationship management (CRM) company.

They're taking advantage of their strongest asset—their relationship with hundreds of thousands of small businesses—to offer them a CRM, SaaS-based product. It's working.

If the strongest asset is the brand, but the business is in structural decline, think seriously about milking the brand until it dies. As much as we humanize them, brands are not people—they are assets to be monetized. Letting one die is only a bad thing if you don't get all the value out of it in its golden years. Too many managers try to Botox their aged brands into a semblance of youth, when they should be letting them go to a profitable hospice. Use those last profits to ease the transition for the real people who made the brand valuable, the employees and customers. In sum, the best that many second-tier players with no rainy-day fund can do is look for a graceful exit that protects employees and doesn't leave customers in the lurch.

## OVERCORRECT

For those with a path to the post-corona future, however narrow, the watchword for how to respond in a crisis is *overcorrect*.

The paradigmatic example is Johnson & Johnson's response to the Tylenol scandal. The reason Johnson & Johnson is one of the most valuable companies in the world is that, in 1982, when a handful of Tylenol bottles were poisoned after leaving the factory, presumably with the intent of extortion, the company didn't say it wasn't their fault and let the police handle it.

Instead, J&J cleared 31 million bottles of Tylenol off the shelves, established a hotline, offered rewards for information about the crime, and replaced purchased bottles. Was the poisoning J&J's fault? No. Did the company overreact? Yes. Did it assure the health of the public and restore the credibility of the company? Yes and yes.

Dr. Mike Ryan, who leads the World Health Organization's Health Emergencies Programme, put it well, a lesson that applies to all emergencies: "If you need to be right before you move, you will never win. Perfection is the enemy of the good when it comes to emergency management. Speed trumps perfection. And the problem we have in society is that everyone is afraid of making a mistake."

For companies in a weak position, survival will depend on radical cost cutting. We are seeing that even with the discovery of a vaccine, getting back to "normal" will be slow and unpredictable. Nearly everyone is facing revenue shortfalls, and companies that won't be getting an infusion of equity capital, cheap debt, or government largesse need to tighten belts like they never have before. There's an old adage in retail: your first markdown is your best markdown. Better to sell something at 80% of your budgeted price than to wait another month and have to dump it at 60%. Waiting to take action only makes the problem worse.

Go through your expenses as a company and as a team. Get to the lowest cost base you can, fast. If you have a landlord, call and say, "I need to suspend payments." Cut compensation, starting with yourself first, then your highest earners—they can afford it, and it sends a message. Find alternative means of compensation—equity, deferred compensation, vacation time—anything that doesn't require cash out the door. There's one exception though: severance. You can't protect jobs, but you can protect people. You have to be fairly Darwinian and harsh around job cuts, but then do everything you can to provide good severance.

Clean up the deadwood. Now is the time to take away the "semi"-retired founder's corner office, cancel the fourth and fifth magazine subscription for the lobby, and tighten up the travel and late-night-meal policy. In June 2020, Microsoft went big on this front, taking a $450 million charge to get out of the brick-and-mortar retail business, a legacy of the Ballmer era.

## GOING ON OFFENSE

Besides cutting costs, where can you do more with the assets you can't shed? I spent a lot of time in summer 2020 on the phone with leaders in higher education who are feeling intense pressure from the pandemic, but because of tenure, strong unions, and facilities, have little cost-cutting flexibility. So what they are doing is trying to decrease their costs per student by reaching more students. A modest investment in technology allows them to expand class sizes without corresponding physical facilities.

For 10 years, I've taught Brand Strategy in the fall to a full auditorium of 160 people at the NYU Stern School of Business. It's a popular class, and more students would take it, but that's our largest classroom. In 2020, however, Stern went virtual, and so that limit was lifted. Now there will be 280 students in my virtual auditorium for Fall 2020. That means some additional fees to Zoom, and we'll hire some additional TAs, but my salary doesn't change, and it doesn't require more Manhattan real estate.

Companies fortunate enough to be in a position of strength should be flexing their pandemic muscles. Microsoft's interest in acquiring TikTok is only the beginning of an M&A (mergers and acquisitions) environment that may be the most robust in a decade. Big tech and the innovator class are playing with fully valued/inflated currency, meaning almost any acquisition is accretive. It takes only a sliver of equity to make a generous stock offer, and cash deals can add more market value by virtue of the multiples new product lines can earn. For example, Lululemon spent $500 million in cash to buy Mirror, and the markets rewarded the company, recognizing the work(out)-from-home movement had leapt a decade, juicing its value $2 billion the next day.

The post-corona world will prize contactless transactions of all kinds. We'll be dumping business travel, business dinners, and business golf (thank god) in favor of more efficient email, phone, and video communication, and what we all need more of—dinner at home and time to unwind. Rethink the benefits you offer your employees—a pet stipend may be more welcome than a gym membership. Flexibility around working from home may be by far the most appreciated perk you can offer. Listening to employees will not only help make the most effective decisions, but it also builds trust, a scarce quantity during a crisis.

Safety and survival are your main goals, and that may mean not just tweaking but entirely rethinking your business model. Are you a restaurant in a nice part of town? That key experience aspect has been severely degraded in favor of safety and convenience. Can you rethink your menu and space so you can offer takeout and "provisions," as one New York restaurant did,[5] still maintaining an air of luxury while being brutally obsessed with survival? Are you a rare books brick and mortar with not much of a website? Time to amp up digital. I got a used book on Amazon that was so well packaged, I had to find the bookseller. I did, and then bought more, directly from their website, because the gift wrap and the experience were so great. In terms of digital, anything you can do to save your customers time will build your NPS (Net Promoter Score) more than flowery marketing language about "these unprecedented times." Cut to the chase, make your site as efficient as possible, save me time.

For every business, this is a good time to forget what you've learned and make the hard changes necessary to position yourself for a post-corona world. Start with a clean sheet of paper.

Freed from legacy decisions, how would you change how you go to market, figure out the right size and composition of your labor force, and decide on your ideal compensation strategies? You get cloud cover to make big decisions, big investments, and bold bets in a global pandemic—no playbook and a lot fewer guardrails.

Where to place those bets? The biggest opportunities will be in areas where the pandemic is accelerating change.

## The Covid Gangster Move: Variable Cost Structures

Cash is great for survival purposes, but the real gangster move is to be capital light, that is, to have a variable cost structure. Uber is the paradigm of this new model. The way the company leverages *other people's assets* is why its share price held its value, despite the near collapse of its core business in the early days of the pandemic. Uber rents space in other people's cars, driven by non-employees (in the eyes of the law, anyway). The second an Uber car stops making the company a profit, it effectively disappears and costs the company nearly nothing. Revenue can go to zero in a crisis, and Uber can take its cost down 60–80%. Hertz, on the other hand, owns its cars and went bankrupt. Boeing has $10 billion in cash, but if its revenue goes down 80%, they can take costs down maybe 10%, maybe

20%. Tesla can furlough its workforce, but it still owes hundreds of millions of dollars on leased properties (factories, retail stores, charging stations), billions of dollars in purchase commitments to feed those factories, health insurance payments for its workforce, and has to provide warranty service on nearly a million Teslas on the road today.

## PHYSICAL ASSET TURNOVER
### GROSS PROFIT/PHYSICAL ASSETS 2019

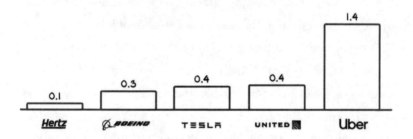

SOURCE: ANALYSIS OF COMPANY FILINGS.

The Uber model is exploitative, to be sure. Uber's "driver partners" still have to make *their* car payments and insurance premiums. The model is akin to United Airlines telling its flight crews to bring their own 747 if they want to get a paycheck. But it's a model that works. For Uber.

Airbnb is another well-positioned player, despite being in an industry that virtually disappeared for a few months. They monetize other people's property, which means someone else is responsible for the mortgage payments. Their business will rebound well, since renting private spaces is going to look attractive long before people are comfortable returning to hotels, amusement parks, or cruise ships. As more and more unemployed people consider joining the gig economy, it will be a good time to rent that extra room, or even move in with your parents for a while and rent your whole apartment.

The gig economy is attractive for the same reasons that it's exploitative. It preys on people who have not been casted into the information economy, as they didn't have access to the requisite credentialing or can't work a traditional job—they might be a caregiver, have a health condition, or just not speak great English. Uber preys on the disenfranchised, and offers subminimum wage work that is flexible and has few start-up costs. Is this a failure of character and code on the part of Uber management and their board, or an indictment on our society, which has allowed these cohorts of vulnerability to form in the millions? The answer is yes.

## The Great Dispersion

Covid-19 is accelerating dispersion across many economic sectors. Amazon, of course, took the store and dispersed it to our front door. Netflix took the movie theater and put it in our living room. We're going to see this dispersion across other industries, including healthcare.

Most people who survived Covid-19 never set foot in a doctor's office. During the pandemic, people with psychological conditions saw their therapists and had medications adjusted without leaving home. This was enabled by changes to insurance rules, which had largely frowned on telemedicine and remote prescribing. Those changes are not likely to be undone, and a flood of innovation and capital will pour into the opportunity well they have drilled. The high-def camera on your mobile phone is a decent diagnostic tool already, but it's a small step to consumer-friendly diagnostic tools arriving on our doorsteps, used, and shipped back. Specialists will be consulted across town, across the country. Teladoc Health, the largest independent U.S. telemedicine service, is adding thousands of doctors to its network.[6] The transition to electronic health records was a major thrust for Obamacare and may be the program's most lasting and important legacy, as electronic records enable a dispersal of an industry ripe for disruption.

We've seen a shift toward dispersion in grocery take place with unheard-of speed. While pre pandemic, most people preferred to pick out their own food, especially produce, stay-at-home advisories have taught us it's okay not to squeeze the avocado. From the beginning of March to the middle of April, online grocery sales increased roughly 90%, while food-delivery sales melted up 50%.[7] The infrastructure this shift has inspired, from warehouses to entrenched customer relationships, will survive the pandemic and change our food system. Habits that should have taken a decade to acquire are a new normal.

## WORKING FROM HOME

Of everything wrought by the pandemic, perhaps the most visible and widespread trend acceleration is the radical transition to working from home. The dispersal of work has arrived. It's a double-edged sword, to be sure. Like so much else in the pandemic, its greatest benefits are being reaped by the already wealthy, who have home office setups, childcare help, or other means of making money during lockdown. Most working-class people, on the other hand, can't do their jobs at home, since they are tied to the store, warehouse, factory, or other place of work. And for those who can do it, it may free us from commutes and office coffee, but it imposes burdens as well.

As a business owner, I've long been skeptical of work-from-home cultures. Ideas need to flirt and fight with one another, and that happens best in person. Just as some things are better said in a phone call than an email, meetings can be more productive and lead to more camaraderie than Zoom calls. Presence is also great for accountability—visual cues help build trust. Also, proximity is key to relationships, which are key to the culture of any organization.

But presence is also expensive. Office space, commuting, dry cleaning, overpriced sandwiches—the costs add up. Meanwhile, the tech that enables virtual interactions keeps getting better and less expensive. The trillion-dollar question is whether tech can disperse our workforce without reducing a culture of innovation and productivity. Six months ago, I still thought it could not. The virus doesn't care about my management theories, however, and so here we are.

Despite stereotypes that telecommuting breeds slacking, early data suggests productivity is up, at least at some companies.[8] As of June 2020, 82% of corporate leaders plan to allow remote working at least some of the time, and 47% say they intend to allow full-time remote work going forward.[9] We are still early in the WFH experiment. High stress levels, distractions from family, and improvised tech aren't a great match. We all have Zoom fatigue, but new tech is emerging that can improve team interactions. We crave contact, but not surveillance. This is a massive opportunity for innovation. Zoom, for instance, announced its first dedicated at-home videoconferencing system, a 27-inch monitor with microphones and wide-angle cameras. The start-up Sidekick offers an always-on tablet aimed at small teams that want constant and spontaneous communication among co-workers, simulating sitting together all day long.[10]

Anecdotally, I think working from home has been harder, not easier, for most people—certainly for parents of young children—and the coveted work-life balance seems further away. But the overwhelming reason for that is that we are also trying to do K–12 school from home, and that's a difficult but likely prospect short-term. As K–12 goes back to 100% in person by 2021, the benefits of WFH will hopefully loom larger (no commuting, no morning rush, less time getting ready, working from several spots in your house).

This is an opportunity for employers to come up with new perks and new ways to support employees. Companies in big cities could spend $2,000 a month for office snacks. (At L2 it was $20,000 a month.) Now that we're not buying those, at my new start-up, Section4, we are giving employees monthly grocery debit cards. They can buy their own snacks. Many people don't have home setups comfortable enough to spend eight to ten hours a day in. Do you do an audit of home office needs and buy a few people good chairs? Do those who already have chairs get a speaker? Do you buy everyone a good mic or just give them gift cards for office supply stores? The options will depend on the size of your team and your budget. The important thing is to show awareness and support.

Working from home on Fridays used to be a perk few people enjoyed. Post corona, working from home on Friday (or Monday, Wednesday, and Friday) will be a new normal.

## SECOND-ORDER EFFECTS OF THE DISPERSION OF WORK

Some retailers stand to benefit. If I'll spend another 10–20% of my waking hours at home, I'll get the great couch from CB2 or invest in Sonos. Home improvement purchases were up 33% in March, even as much of the country went into lockdown— if people are going to be stuck in their homes, working from home, it's time to tackle those home improvement projects.

The normalization of work from home may help create

greater opportunities for women. Women under 30 who don't have children have closed the pay gap with their male counterparts. Once women have kids, they go to 77 cents on the dollar relative to their male counterparts. Part of our ability to create the same career trajectory for women with kids is to create more options and flexibility around where they work from. Part of working from home is the ability to work at different hours than the rest of your team, allowing for family needs like caretaking, side gigs, or hobbies that contribute to a work-life balance. It may be time to unroll the yoga mat or dust off the drum set in the garage, instead of spending 225 hours, or 9 full days, a year commuting.[11]

However, there are risks to working from home. If your big tech job can be moved to Denver, there's a decent chance it can be moved to Bangalore. Also, as great as it is to work from your couch, we are an unequal society in which women still do more housework and caretaking than men. As a result, especially as schools are reluctant to reopen, if extended childcare or home-schooling is required, the more likely parent to drop out of work will be the woman. This is especially true for the lower income brackets.

Career advancement is often the result of in-person, informal communications, like drinks after work or impromptu lunches. Presence has implications for who is top of mind for a promotion, or whom an executive is most familiar and comfortable with. This calls for companies to make extra efforts to include employees working from home in meetings, informal communications, and advancement decisions. Judge performance, not the schedule.

Even with the best efforts, it will be difficult to avoid a disparity in opportunities between those who can come to the office five (or more) days a week, and those who cannot, whether because of childcare or other dependent-care obligations (more likely to be women), because they are immunocompromised, or because they live a thousand miles away. This is unfair to employees, but it's an employer's loss—the very obstacles that interfere with office attendance can forge skills and discipline. In the nine firms I've founded, my experience has been that employees who are also mothers have often mastered a level of efficiency that noticeably outstrips their peers who are fathers.

I'll talk more about this in chapter 5, but we can't ignore the fact that remote work will be a means of increased income inequality. Sixty percent of jobs that pay over $100,000 can be done from home, compared to only 10% of those that pay under $40,000. This is a major contributor to the pandemic's disparate impact across income levels (low-income workers are nearly four times as likely to have been laid off or furloughed as high-income workers). Post corona, the benefits of increased flexibility that come with remote work alternatives will flow to the already well off.

There's an intra-class dynamic here as well, though this is more about comfort than fundamental inequality. Working from home can mean a lot of different things. Senior people with big houses in the suburbs have dedicated office rooms and equipment, many have even worked out full-time childcare, or their kids are old enough they don't need constant supervision. Junior people, on the other hand, are more likely to live in cramped apartments and starter homes that don't have dedicated workspaces.

Those frustrations spell opportunity, however. The same tech that enables working from home also enables working from satellite and temporary offices. I was, to put it mildly, a WeWork bear,[12] but I'm actually bullish on the underlying concept. Flexible spaces where people can work alone or in teams, distributed throughout cities and beyond, sounds like the future.

The second-order effects of a shift toward much more working from home—or working from remote offices—are fascinating. What happens to cities in a world where you don't need to live in them?

It's a trend worth watching, but I wouldn't write the obituary of cities just yet. Forty years ago, it was fashionable to predict the death of the city, but they came roaring back, and not because people had to live in them for their jobs. Young people brought cities back because they wanted to live near other young people and to get access to culture and entertainment. Indeed, those draws have proven so strong that many cities, New York first among them, have become so desirable that young people—in many cases the children of those who saved cities in the first place—can no longer afford to live there. Best case, we see the midlife professional move out to leafy, charming villages with great schools, and let the twentysomethings come back to the Village.

# The Brand Age Gives Way to the Product Age

At my first firm, Prophet, we roamed the world preaching to Global 500 companies that a firm's ability to provide above-market returns depended on their ability to develop a compelling brand identity, and then treat this ID as a religion, nodding to the identity with every action and investment. And the way that was done was through the awesome power of broadcast advertising.

From the end of WWII until the introduction of Google, the gangster algorithm for shareholder value was simple—create an average, mass-produced product and infuse it with intangible associations. You then reinforce those associations through cheap broadcast media, which occupied the average American for five hours a day. The Brand Age grabbed the baton from an out-of-breath manufacturing sector. Firms like McKinsey, Goldman Sachs, and Omnicom built the workforce and infrastructure for a booming services economy. The Brand Age created gurus, marketing departments, and CMOs, and kept black town cars lined around the headquarters of Viacom and Condé Nast. Emotion injected into a mediocre product (American cars, light beer, cheap food) was the algorithm for creating hundreds of billions in stakeholder value. Kodak moments and "teaching the world to sing"[13] translated to irrational margins based on an emotional response to inanimate products.

Don Draper lived the high life. The ad business saw creatives who dyed their hair in their forties and wore cool glasses as the messiahs of the last half of the twentieth century. The ad industry brought brand to washing machine and minivan manufacturers. Brand was a new kind of pixie dust that offered an exceptional lifestyle to average businesspeople. Believers in the advertising industrial complex would be blessed with sacrosanct margins despite products void of differentiation.

I made a nice living preaching this. And then . . . the internet.

I sold my stake in Prophet in 2002. I had started hating the services industry. Success in the services industry is a function of your ability to communicate ideas and develop relationships. I loved the former and despised the latter—managing colleagues and being friends with people for money. The services industry is prostitution, minus the dignity. If you spend a lot of time at dinners with people who aren't your family, it means you're selling something that is mediocre.

I got lucky and got out. The Brand Age was drawing to a close. There's no one moment, but a series of opportunistic infections: Google, Facebook, and technology that liberated the affluent from ads. If you want to mark the beginning of the end, you could do worse than Tivo. Launched, fittingly, in the last few months of the twentieth century, Tivo allowed those with extra disposable income to trade it for something even more valuable: their time. Once you owned a Tivo, with just a little patience and prior planning, you never had to watch a commercial again. Advertising became a tax that only the poor and technologically illiterate had to pay.

Just as Tivo was giving us a preview of a world without commercials (at least for those who could afford it) a slew of other new products were coming along that were ridiculously better than what we used before (Google vs. classified ads, Kayak vs. travel agents, Spotify vs. CDs). They don't need to interrupt *Succession* every ten minutes.

If Tivo marks the beginning of the shift from the Brand Age to the Product Age, the summer of 2020 saw the Brand Age's end. The killing of George Floyd and subsequent protests briefly displaced the pandemic in the front and center of our national consciousness, making obvious the passing of the Brand Age into history. Seemingly every brand company did what they always do when America's sins are pulled out from the back of the closet where we try to keep them hidden: they called up their agencies and posted inspiring words, arresting images, and black rectangles. Message: We care. Only this time, it didn't resonate. Their brand magic fizzled.

First on social media, then tumbling from there onto newspapers and evening news, activists and customers started using the tools of the new age to compare these companies' carefully crafted brand messages with the reality of their operations. "This you?"

became the Twitter meme that exposed the brand wizards. Companies who posted about their "support" for black empowerment were called out when their own websites revealed the music did not match the words. The NFL claimed it celebrates protest, and the internet tweeted back, "This you?" under a picture of Colin Kaepernick kneeling. L'Oréal posted that "speaking out is worth it" and got clapped back with stories about dropping a model just three years earlier for speaking out against racism. The performative wokeness across brands felt forced and hollow. Systemic racism is a serious issue, and a 30-second spot during *The Masked Singer* doesn't prove you are serious about systemic racism. That's always been true, about ads on any issue, but social media and the ease of access to data on the internet has made it much harder for companies to pretend.

## WELCOME TO THE PRODUCT AGE

Paying lip service to social causes is a sideline for brand builders, of course, but those digital tools are damaging the core business as well. In the Brand Age, a wealthy traveler new in town tells his cabdriver to take him to the Ritz, because that's the brand he knows. In the Product Age, this valuable customer checks her phone as she gets off the plane, learns that the Ritz is being renovated, and that reviewers believe it's overpriced, and she crowdsources a recommendation for a new boutique hotel in a hipper neighborhood.

The losers in this transition are the media companies that provided platforms for the big and bold brand-building advertising of the Brand Age, and the creative-driven ad agencies that made them. If you make your living on the back of 30-second spots featuring award-winning ad copy and talented actors connecting emotions to products, this is not the future you were hoping for. Twenty years ago, Levi Strauss & Co. asked three outside advisers to sit in on their board meetings: two advertising agency icons, Lee Clow and Nigel Bogle, and yours truly, the brand strategist. That's how important creative and advertising was to the company. I've been in perhaps 150 board meetings since those Levi's days, and I don't think I've heard a director ask what the ad agency thought about anything. Their time has passed.

## STOCK PERFORMANCE OF FACEBOOK, GOOGLE, AND THE OLD GUARD
AUGUST 2015–AUGUST 2020

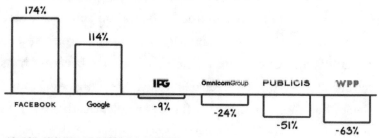

SOURCE: ANALYSIS OF SEEKING ALPHA DATA.

Troubled economic times always mean a pullback in ad dollars, and that is initially affecting the online and traditional players. Search terms and ads on Google and Facebook plunged 20% in the month after George Floyd's killing. But the pullback in traditional media was even steeper. The recovery will be equally bloody. Because when the tide comes back in, it will flow only to the advertising media of the Product Age, not the old guard of the Brand Age. The Google-Facebook duopoly's share of the digital ad market is predicted at 61% in 2021.[14]

In 2012, I was doing work with the Four Seasons. Great firm—nice people, Canadian (redundant). During the Great Recession, the luxury hotel brand had to cease all print advertising as revenue per room had declined 25%. And a strange thing happened when demand returned: the absence of print marketing didn't seem to make any difference. Multiply this phenomenon by a million, and you have what will happen—thousands of the biggest advertisers globally are about to use this forced abstinence from broadcast media (with business down 30–50%) to kick the habit, and never return.

The two largest radio firms, iHeartRadio and Cumulus Media, will likely be Chapter 11 (again) by summer 2021. Radio advertising is projected to decline 14% in 2020.[15] Covid-19 has a mortality rate of 0.5–1% in the U.S.[16] Among U.S. media firms, the death rate will be ten times higher. Firms ranging from Condé Nast to Viacom have furloughed and laid off people as Facebook and Google have ramped up hiring. How do you identify the best people at News Corp, Time Warner, and Condé Nast? Simple, they will soon be working at Google.

Even harder hit are the digital marketing firms that aren't

## PRE- VS. POST-CORONAVIRUS US 2020 AD SPENDING FORECAST
DECEMBER 2019 VS. MARCH 2020
☐ DEC 19    ▨ MAR 20

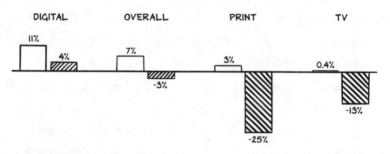

SOURCE: MAGNA GLOBAL.

Facebook or Google. BuzzFeed and Yelp have seen display ads on site decline 40–70% in 2020 vs. 2019 and are in the ICU. *Vox, HuffPo,* and *Vice* will follow. Some will make it out. Some.

## Red and Blue

There are two fundamental business models. **One,** a company can sell stuff for more than the cost of making it. Apple takes about $400 worth of circuits and glass, imbues it with the promise of status and sex appeal through brilliant advertising, and charges me $1,200 for an iPhone. **Two,** a company can give stuff away—or sell it below cost—and charge other companies for access to its product: the consumer's behavioral data. NBC hires

Jerry Seinfeld to write a TV show, films dozens of episodes on a studio lot in LA made to look like a sanitized version of Manhattan, then beams it out for free to anyone with a subscription to watch. But every eight minutes, NBC interrupts the witty banter with several minutes of ads, for which it charges the advertisers, who are its actual customers. The product, of course, is you.

Some businesses combine both. The NFL gets about a third of its revenue from the first model: selling tickets to fans at the games and selling clothes and other items with NFL logos on it. And it gets about two-thirds of its revenue from selling access to those fans to advertisers, from 5-million-dollar Super Bowl ads to the corporate logos plastered over every available square foot in the stadium.

As we move into a tech-based economy, however, that second business model becomes both more lucrative and more troubling. In the old days of advertising, we only had to give up some of our time and attention to get the free stuff the advertising paid for. But when our relationships are online, the companies giving us this supposedly free stuff suddenly have all this data about us—what we read, where we shop, who we talk to, what we eat, where we live. And they are using that data to make more money off of us. **We used to trade time for value. Now we trade our privacy for value.**

Furthermore, the companies that accumulate this data are getting more sophisticated at using it to capture more of our data, and more of our time. NBC could only send out one program at a time, and it had to do its best to gauge what mix of programming over the course of the week would net it the most valuable audience to sell to its advertisers. But Facebook can customize its programming for every single one of its advertising attention resource units (what you and I call "people") to keep them clicking through screens, thus generating more inventory for Facebook's advertising machine.

Industries will increasingly bifurcate along this line of division. We've already seen this in mobile. Android versus iOS offers you a choice between a decent product for low or no upfront cost, but the sacrifice of your data and privacy, versus a higher quality, better-branded product, for much more cash up front, but much less exploitation on the back end. Android phones poll 1,200 data points a day from their users and send that back to the Google data-mining mother ship. iOS phones pull 200, and Apple bends over backward to emphasize that data is not being used for profiteering. "The truth is," Apple CEO Tim Cook said in 2018, "we could make a ton of money if we monetized our customers, if we made our customers our product. We've elected not to do that."[17]

The entire world is bifurcating into Android or iOS. Android users are the masses who trade privacy for value. iOS are the wealthy who enjoy the luxury of privacy and status signaling by shelling out $1,249 plus tax (more than one month's household income in Hungary) in exchange for $443 in sensors and chipsets (what it costs to make an iPhone).[18]

You can get your video entertainment on YouTube for free, but it's a mishmash of content, and the algorithm that is supposed to help you sort through it pushes you toward whatever retains your interest. And unless you're a modern-day saint, there's a good chance you'll be served inflammatory, provocative content, whether it's conspiracy theories, violence, or political extremism. Google tracks your views, associates it with everything else it knows about you (quite a lot), and uses all that data to sell ads to you and the many cohorts you are part of.

Netflix, on the other hand, operates a blue/iOS model. You pay, and you get content. You are the customer, and the content is excellent. YouTube, on the other hand, is worse in quality but free—if you don't mind the data mining and the chance your children will be turned into white nationalists.

Expect this divide to deepen as the two models become increasingly incompatible. The NFL can operate in both worlds, since its advertising revenue streams don't undermine the premise of its ticket and merchandise streams. The same isn't true for a company like Apple, however. Tim Cook has promised us that Apple won't harvest our data. "Privacy is a fundamental human right," he said. But Apple receives $12 billion a year for making Google the default search engine for iOS. Apple will likely divorce from Google, even though it will cost them $12 billion a year, plus the billions it will take to build or buy their own search engine. Apple will not be able to monetize search to nearly the same extent as Google, since it can't make Tim into a liar. But they can survive without Google. Just as they can get us to watch *Murphy Brown* at $15 million per episode (*The Morning Show*), they'll be able to shove a search engine that's

80% as good as Google down our throats. They own the rails. I know, you're thinking they need to do a better job with maps first. Fair point.

## RED AND BLUE SOCIAL MEDIA

Right now, social media is all red in terms of their approach to data vs. privacy. Free services, grossly exploitative, sometimes in ways we don't even realize. In June 2020, it was revealed that TikTok scans the user's clipboard every few seconds, even when the app is running in the background.[19] The company promised to stop doing this (after a new iOS security feature caught it in the act), but if you used TikTok before the summer of 2020, you can assume that everything you've copied and pasted on your phone since you started using the app is now stored on a database in China under your name. Using Facebook might not get your personal data uploaded to the CCCP's cloud, but given Facebook's track record of protecting the privacy of its users, that's only because the Chinese will be outbid by a Ukrainian teenager juiced up on bitcoin and looking to bring down democracy.

There's a huge opportunity here for one or even several players to become the iOS of social media. The best opportunity to go blue, and capture a smaller but more valuable audience, is Twitter's. Twitter has been trying to take the red/Android pill, but it isn't working. And while management insists on losing money trying to exploit users by building another rage machine, those users are exploiting Twitter to build their own brands and businesses. It's time for Twitter to come over to the blue/iOS world and start charging for value. Twitter doesn't have the scale to compete on an ad model, and their ad tools are substandard.

After months of public lobbying on this front by a brave (and handsome!) NYU Stern professor of marketing,[20] Twitter finally announced in July 2020 that it would "explore" a subscription model. The market loved it. Despite Twitter's admission, in the very same earnings call, that ad revenue had dropped 23%, the stock was up 10%. If Twitter had a full-time CEO, they would have come to this conclusion in half the time.

I can save Twitter another year of "exploring" the subscription model. Subscription fees should be based on the number of followers. If @kyliejenner can earn $430,000 per promoted tweet, she'll pay $10,000 a month to maintain her revenue stream, and @karaswisher (1.3 million followers), I'm pretty sure, would pay $250 a month. Verified accounts with <2,000 followers would remain free to maintain critical mass.

The B2B market alone would be huge, as Twitter has replaced PR, news agencies, and IR firms. What firm wouldn't pay $2,000 a month to announce their new SaaS/diet/keto/hemp product? Twitter could take a 40% hit to top-line revenue over the short term, and triple their stock in the next twenty-four months as they move to subscription.

Going vertical would buttress the subscription offering. Twitter should acquire several of the remaining independent media properties (Lee, McClatchy, Condé Nast, Hearst, etc.) or assets from them.

The subscription model offers a free gift with purchase—identity. People are less awful when their name and reputation are attached. Ad-supported platforms are incentivized to allow bots and Russian interference, and to provide more oxygen to ideas that lack merit but are incendiary. Rage equals engagement, which translates to more Nissan ads. Remember that time when Netflix or LinkedIn really pissed you off? That was Twitter or Facebook.

Also, Twitter has the added benefit of being terrible at advertising. A move to a subscription model would forfeit dramatically less revenue than Facebook, which monetizes users at a higher rate than Twitter.[21] Twitter could also hold on to much of their ad revenue during the transition phase, or even settle on a hybrid model that cleans up 90% of the carcinogens.

While Twitter is figuring this out at half-CEO speed, Microsoft should launch their own microblogging platform as a sub-brand of LinkedIn. If there is any doubt that media is nicotine (addictive) but advertising is what gives us cancer (tobacco), compare and contrast the most successful media firms of the last decade: Google, Facebook, Netflix, and LinkedIn. Two are tearing at the fabric of society, the other two . . . are not. The difference? Facebook and Google run on rage as an engagement model; Netflix and LinkedIn are powered on a subscription model (note: approximately 20% of LinkedIn revenues come from advertising).[22]

LinkedIn is much of the great taste of Twitter, an interesting feed full of connections and discovery, without the
calories—bots pumping Tesla, death and rape threats, and anti-
vaxers. LinkedIn is the social media platform we're all hoping
Facebook and Twitter would become.

## RED AND BLUE SEARCH AND BEYOND

Search has also been red, but blue search is coming. Apple's
proprietary iOS search is inevitable. Expect Apple to buy Duck-
DuckGo or roll out their own soon. Beyond that, Sridhar Ramas-
wamy, former head of Google's ad business, recently launched
Neeva, a new Google competitor that will be using a subscription model. On the company's website, one of the first links is for
a bill of rights: "Your information belongs to you." If you are
willing to pay for it. Neeva recognizes the soft costs of Google
may have created a white space for the anti-Google Google.

Likewise, the most innovative firm of the last decade seized
on Amazon's abuse of their customers (third-party retailers).
Shopify's value proposition is simple, and powerful: we are your
partner. You control the data, the branding, and custody of the
consumer. Brand building is the science of building goodwill
that can be monetized. A lot of innovation is monetizing ill will.
In this case, Amazon had abused their power to such an extent, they created an opportunity the size of Ottawa. Shopify's
is now worth as much as Boeing and Airbus combined.

Expect to see this divide emerge in more and more industries. Low-cost players from airlines to fast food will seek to take advantage of customer data and pass the savings on to their advertising resource units . . . oops, I mean customers. Premium players will wrap themselves in the blue flag of privacy and collect a nice margin for the courtesy of not exploiting their customers' data.

# [ 2 ]

# THE FOUR

March through July of 2020 saw more than half a million deaths from Covid-19, including more than 150,000 in the United States. A lockdown meant to contain the virus did nothing of the kind, but left in its wake at least a recession, possibly a depression. Dozens of household-name companies filed for bankruptcy. The unemployment rate tripled, hitting an all-time high in April.

Over the same five-month period, nine major tech companies increased in market value by $1.9 *trillion*. And they weren't any five months, but the worst five-month stretch the world has experienced in nearly a century. These are not drug companies or healthcare companies, which might be expected to benefit from the outbreak of a global disease. Some of these companies, notably Amazon and Netflix, do get some specific

## GROWTH IN MARKET CAPITALIZATION
MARCH 2 – JULY 31, 2020

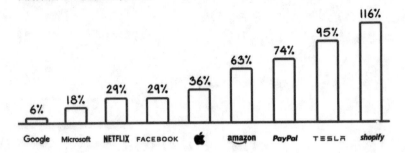

SOURCE: ANALYSIS OF SEEKING ALPHA DATA.

revenue enhancements from the lockdowns, of course, but that should not exclude them from the brutal headwinds of a slowing or shrinking economy. Likewise, an increase in online shopping benefits PayPal and Shopify, but to shop people need money, jobs, and optimism—all in short supply in the pandemic. And in what universe does the closure of business and the suppression of travel benefit a company that makes high-end automobiles? Nor is this simply the result of central bank activity or some new species of financialization that has divorced the stock market from economy reality.

We are witnessing the rise to dominance of a subset of American companies. In chapter 1, I wrote about the limited scope of the stock market recovery, and how it has largely accrued to big companies. But that's only half the story. Even within the big companies, one group stands alone. Big tech.

The major indexes with the tech leaders removed were *down*

at the 2020 halfway point. Outside of technology, even many of the lions of American capitalism have been declawed: shares in ExxonMobil, Coca-Cola, JPMorgan Chase, Boeing, Disney, and 3M were down 30% halfway through the year, for an aggregate loss of market capitalization of nearly half a trillion dollars.

One sector has outdone all the others in the pandemic: big tech. Tech leaders from Netflix to Shopify, and tech-adjacent Tesla, have done exceptionally well. The biggest of the bunch are the companies I call "the Four" (Amazon, Apple, Facebook, and Google), along with Microsoft. These five were up 24% at the 2020 midpoint, with an aggregate market capitalization *gain* of over $1.1 trillion. By mid-August, their year-to-date return had soared to 47%, for a gain of $2.3 trillion. Their combined heft is unprecedented.[1] **These five companies make up 21% of the value of all publicly traded U.S. companies.**

## INDEXED STOCK PERFORMANCE OF FIVE LARGEST FIRMS IN S&P 500 VS. S&P 500
JANUARY – JULY, 2020

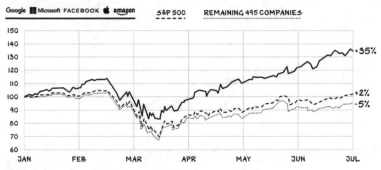

SOURCE: FACTSET, GOLDMAN SACHS GLOBAL INVESTMENT RESEARCH.

Conclusion: It's big tech's world. We just live in it.

The dominance of big tech is not a surprise. I wrote a book about it in 2017 (*The Four*), and I was neither the first nor the last to make the point. Often, those observations came with a caveat: what goes up must come down. The rapid rise of these companies must mean that there's froth in their stock price, and that when the music stopped, they would come down just as fast as they rose.

Nope.

As with so much else, the pandemic has taken this trend—the increasing dominance of our lives and economy by just a few tech companies—and accelerated it ten years. In no small part that's because of the dynamics I identified in the last chapter: the market is rewarding winners like never before. But the winners in big tech are being rewarded to an even greater degree because their advantages are even greater. This is most true with respect to the Four. The rest of these companies, led by Microsoft and Netflix, share some of the advantages of the Four. Here's how they've turned a world crisis into an opportunity to get bigger, stronger, and more dominant.

## The Power of Bigness / The Monopoly Algorithm / Featurization

People often ask me what stocks I own. My investing advice is simple: I only invest in unregulated monopolies. They aren't supposed to exist, but our antitrust laws were written in the era of steam engines, and enforcement has been nonexistent. Big tech is the twenty-first century version of John D. Rockefeller and Andrew Carnegie, and there is no trust-busting Teddy Roosevelt on the horizon to rein them in. Not on our horizon anyway—Margrethe Vestager, you are my hero.

How have they done it? The algorithm is this: innovate, obfuscate, and exploit.

Tech monopolies are founded on innovation: Amazon has figured out a thousand tricks for selling goods cheap and getting them to you fast. Apple made a phone that was so much better than everyone else's, they spent the next decade suing the competition for blatantly ripping it off. Google realized the key to search was to leverage links, and Facebook made social media into a social network. All of these companies saw daylight and dashed ahead before anyone else.

Once they got into the open field, however, they turned their attention toward protecting their advantage. Defending a market is far easier than creating a new one. How do they do this? Obfuscate. Conceal their monopolistic position with gauzy promotional videos bubbling with buzzwords and extolling their boy genius founder, while pouring millions into K Street lobbying operations and public relations schmoozing. Make CNBC into their bitch and treat the Department of Justice like an annoying kid brother. All to obfuscate the fact that they long ago stopped being scrappy upstarts and are now sitting on geysers of cash generated by their core businesses, in which they face little serious competition. It used to be that when one company took over an industry, we called that a monopoly, and the antitrust police came and broke up the party. The monopolists of big tech have beat the system.

Having fended off the normal limits on market power, they can enjoy the fruits by exploiting their privileged position. At the core of these businesses is a flywheel. In physics, a flywheel is a rotating disk that stores kinetic energy in its momentum, and then spins that energy out to a nearby engine. In the context of business, as the flywheel rotates it increases output or revenue without increasing input or cost. The ultimate flywheel is Amazon Prime. Amazon Prime attracts shoppers who want a wide assortment of products with rapid fulfillment. These subscribers also enjoy the benefits of services like Amazon Prime Video, which increase the stickiness of Prime and time spent on the platform. It's no surprise that Walmart launched their own competitive service, Walmart+. The only mystery is why it took so long.

Once you have a monopoly and your flywheel is spun up, network effects, cheap capital, idolatry of innovators, and a feckless DOJ and FTC have resulted in a monopoly era in which a wildly profitable business (phones, digital marketing, loyalty programs, cloud, Yoda dolls) can generate such staggering value ("antimatter") that entire industries become loss leaders ("features") to differentiate and protect the antimatter. Netscape, the fastest-growing software firm in history, went from antimatter to feature when Microsoft began bundling Internet Explorer with Office.

The Four aren't the only companies with a flywheel. In 2016, when Walmart acquired Jet.com for $3.3 billion, I said it was a bad deal. Okay, I said it was "a $3.5 billion hair transplant on a midlife-crisis Walmart." I was right about Jet as a business—Walmart announced it was shutting Jet down in May 2020. But I was wrong about it as a Walmart acquisition. It dramatically increased Walmart's percentage of online sales. And the market values online sales much more highly than brick-and-mortar, since that's where the growth is, where the data is, and where the future is. Just by buying Jet, Walmart went from 6% to 16% of sales online. Even though, in isolation, Jet.com wasn't likely worth $3 billion, it was worth $3 billion to Walmart. And the wisdom of the markets has borne out. At the time of the acquisition, Walmart's ecommerce growth was slowing, but after the deal, and since it put Jet.com founder and CEO Marc Lore in charge of its entire ecommerce operation, online sales are up 176%.[2] And Walmart's stock price has nearly doubled.

## IT'S ALL TECH NOW

The power of technology and featurization is changing everything. "Tech" used to be a narrowly defined industry consisting of companies that made computer hardware and software, which companies in "other" industries bought for their business. Even in the dot-com era, we recognized disruptors, but we thought of them as new players in "other" industries. Pets.com was a pet store, just online. Broadcast.com was a radio network, just online. E-Trade was a brokerage, just online.

Amazon was a bookstore, just online.

Except it wasn't, not at all. Amazon was, is, and always will be a technology company. What Jeff Bezos knew all along was that very soon, technology companies would no longer merely make technology infrastructure for other firms. Instead, technology companies would be in those businesses themselves.

In the 2000s, we started to see Bezos's vision come to life. Amazon expanded from books to general merchandise to movies and television shows, to groceries, to consumer electronics, to cloud computing services. Likewise, Google distributes movies, makes home automation equipment, phones, and healthcare products. Apple's phone was so successful that the company dropped "Computer" from its name, and now it's producing television shows.

From the outside, companies including Airbnb, Uber, Compass, and Lemonade look like rental agents, ride-hailing services, real estate agents, and insurance companies. But in fact, these are technology companies, differing only by the analog industry they've chosen to deploy their technology against.

How are they able to do this? In part, it's better technology—online relationships, algorithms, and data—a better way to run any business. Whatever your widget, you can make more of them for cheaper, and sell more of them for higher margins, if you build your business from the ground up to be online and data driven. But the companies that figured this out early and capitalized (the Four—Amazon, Apple, Facebook, and Google) now have an equally powerful advantage: size. With their lower cost of capital, monopoly power, and bulk, they are herding every business toward tech.

## THE FOUR EXPAND EVERYWHERE

Some examples. First, delivery. Amazon has decided it wants to own the delivery business. So, it's going to turn what used to be an industry (delivery), into a feature (Prime). Jeff Bezos, a few billion dollars, and a team of engineers could give FedEx a run for its money. At least it would be a fair fight. But Bezos is not fighting the least bit fair. He helms an online retailer that reaches into 82% of American households, provides online commerce for everyone from Bucks4Books to Gucci, and generates $17 million in sales a minute.[3] And he's pointed that market power at FedEx.

Amazon is better at FedEx's own game: its on-time delivery rate is better, its prices (for delivering third-party goods sold on Amazon) are lower, and Amazon is investing to extend its lead, moving to one-day shipping on more and more items in more and more markets. FedEx shareholders have woken up in an M. Night Shyamalan nightmare. Instead of seeing dead people, investors are haunted by Mercedes-Benz Sprinter vans with an arrow the shape of a smile on their side. Everywhere. They might as well be German Panzer tanks fighting a white-and-purple cavalry of FedEx trucks. There will be a lot of macho

## SHARE OF U.S. HOUSEHOLDS
2020

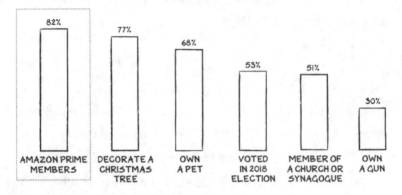

SOURCES: CONSUMER INTELLIGENCE RESEARCH PARTNERS, CHRISTMAS TREE
ASSOCIATION, U.S. ELECTIONS PROJECT, CENSUS BUREAU, PEW RESEARCH.

battle cries from FedEx, some heroism, and an increasing stench of death. (Can't help it, I love WWII war metaphors.)

Another example: wearables.

Apple is dominating wearables, a category that has existed for hundreds of years, only we didn't know it had a name. How dominant? From inception five years ago, Apple is now the largest player in the watch business—by a factor of four.

Apple's ability to grow its services and wearables business speaks to Tim Cook's management acumen—the firm is now getting nearly half its revenues from something other than the iPhone. Apple's wearables business (Apple Watch, AirPods, and Beats) alone generated over $20 billion in revenue in 2019, making it bigger than McDonald's.[4] If spun, which it should be (if we had an FTC or DOJ), the business would likely be one of the

## REVENUE
2019

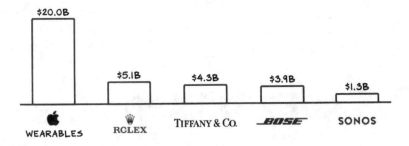

SOURCE: COMPANY FILINGS, IMORE.

20 most valuable firms in the world. But as smart as Cook is, and as good at designing glass rectangles as Jony Ive was (talk about leveraging a core competency), if you think that's how Apple will sell $20 billion worth of watches and headphones this year, you're not paying attention. **It's the flywheel.** Rolex makes a beautiful watch, but I don't have a Rolex phone in my pocket for it to connect to. Bose makes amazing headphones, but it doesn't have 500 temples to the brand (stores) where customers try them on among the hippest crowd in the world. Congratulations, wearables, you're now tech.

## THE FOUR COME TO HOLLYWOOD

One more example: streaming media.

Jack Warner, cofounder of Warner Brothers, built a 13,600-square-foot Georgian-style mansion in Hollywood in the 1930s.

It was often the site of a who's who of the golden age of Holly-wood, the archetypal studio mogul's estate. Now this estate belongs to Jeff Bezos.

What tech has done to retail is unfolding in media. This jug-gernaut of an industry, with hundreds of billions in value and cultural influence like no other industry in the world, is being *featurized*—made into a feature, an accessory, to sell batteries and toilet paper. Granted, it's sort of always done that (e.g., Bud Light commercials).

Streaming video adds momentum to the flywheel. Movies and entertainment evoke powerful emotions. The NPS score (consumers' emotional connection to a company) is negative to zero for ecommerce and internet companies, but it's strong for SVOD (streaming video on demand) companies. Loving *Flea-bag* means you're more likely to buy your next toaster from Amazon, not Target or Williams-Sonoma.

Large entertainment media firms (Comcast, AT&T, Verizon, Fox, Sony) will cede value to Amazon and Apple—two tech gi-ants for whom media is not a core business, but just a part of the flywheel, a feature. Similar to Walmart, Disney is the only incumbent with the assets, leadership, and shareholder base to land counterpunches on the purveyors of paper towels and AirPods.

The shift in value has already started. In the 13-month period between January 2019 and February 2020, Apple and Amazon *added* Disney, AT&T/Time Warner, Fox, Netflix, Comcast, Viacom, MGM, Discovery, and Lionsgate to their market capitalization. Read the last sentence again.

## CHANGE IN APPLE & AMAZON MARKET CAP VS. MARKET CAP OF MEDIA COMPANIES
### JANUARY – AUGUST 12, 2020

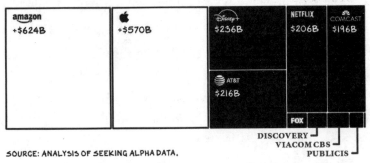

SOURCE: ANALYSIS OF SEEKING ALPHA DATA.

Netflix is balanced on the knife edge of this divide. As recently as late 2019, Netflix was still the lead dog in the streaming pack, with the best content, the best technology, a huge first-mover advantage in subscribers, and hall-of-fame management.[5] And it's still a very big dog. Netflix is perhaps the only other company to have accomplished what Amazon has pulled off by convincing the markets to essentially give them a blank check for customer acquisition and infrastructure investment on the strength of a vision. And the company has benefited from the pandemic: stock is up 50% since January, and subscriber growth is up 110% in the first half of 2020, double the growth of the same period last year.[6] If Netflix continues to increase its content budget at the same rate, by 2025 Netflix will spend more on *Stranger Things, You, The Crown,* and other original content than the U.S. spends on food stamps (SNAP). Who says capitalism isn't working?

But you know who is not impressed by those numbers? The guy taking human growth hormone in Jack Warner's mansion. Bezos has himself a flywheel. So does Tim Cook. Reed Hastings might be their equal as a CEO, but he's missing their strategic advantage. Netflix likely needs to bulk up. First move is to acquire Spotify, another pursuer of the throne with great assets and potentially fatal weaknesses. Together, they snatch up Sonos, and have music and video, along with a physical presence in the home to help fend off Alexa and Siri. That would give Netflix even more daylight.

Other players that emerged in the streaming video space—Quibi and Peacock—are late to the party. Peacock has a complex value proposition (tiered offerings), and many of NBC's shows are available on other platforms. Quibi . . . it's sad to see two brilliant business minds screw up so bad. As *Wired* put it, laughing at Quibi is way more fun than watching Quibi.[7] Neither has a flywheel or a value proposition strong enough to justify another monthly subscription.

Media has become a customer acquisition vehicle vs. a stand-alone business. So, the firms with the most seamless means of speedballing the media crack will win. The Four already have an IV hooked up to your arm, why not let them add video to it? Worth noting: Jack Warner, the original owner of Bezos's LA mansion, was subject to antitrust action by the DOJ in 1948.

One way to know when big tech is seriously threatening established players is when the established players forget what made them great and start doing dumb things. Cue HBO Max.

Television is the defining art form of our age. Movies have gotten boring and predictable. Who wants another superhero sequel? The pinnacle of cinematic creativity is television, and HBO has been the best of TV for decades. *The Sopranos, The Wire, Six Feet Under, Sex and the City, Game of Thrones* . . . HBO is the brand of unrivaled creative genius. HBO wins an Emmy for every $75 million it spends on content, versus Amazon at $400 million. Apple's *The Morning Show* costs $15 million per episode[8]—more than HBO spent per episode of *Game of Thrones*.[9] Which would you rather watch? Tough call. The last sentence is a lie.

What does AT&T CEO John Stankey do with the AT&T/WarnerMedia acquisition of HBO? He walks into the Musée d'Orsay, this jewel of a museum in Paris, and says, "Let's scale this." HBO used to be the best luxury brand in content, the Birkin bag of streaming video. Now it's an expensive catchall at $15 a month. That's double the cost of Disney+ and three times

## CONTENT SPEND PER EMMY
2019

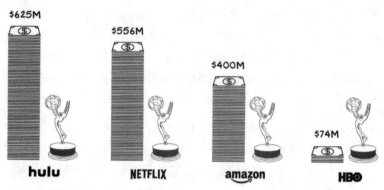

$625M — **hulu**
$556M — **NETFLIX**
$400M — **amazon**
$74M — **HBO**

SOURCE: ANALYSIS OF OBSERVER DATA.

the cost of Apple TV+. Nobody wants to pay $15 for a bundle that has *The Big Bang Theory*. And to make sure the rollout is a complete mess, HBO Max isn't available on Roku and Amazon Fire TV, because leadership failed to secure distribution deals for the most popular streaming device (Roku), which together with Amazon Fire TV accounts for 70% of streaming video viewership.[10]

Who sees opportunity in HBO's blunders? Apple. The Cupertino firm is investing $6 billion in original, vertical content on Apple TV+, seizing the luxury positioning from HBO. **Luxury is about artisanship and scarcity.** Apple TV+ isn't about what's on Apple TV+, but what *isn't*. Specifically, nothing that isn't produced by Apple. Sure, *The Morning Show* is no *Sex and the City*, but neither was HBO's *Arliss*. HBO spent years ramping up its original content before *Sex and the City* (1998), and *The Sopranos*

(1999) made it the prestige TV champ. When you wonder where all of Apple's $6 billion in content spend went, remember, the first iPhone didn't even have apps.

## Bigger Tech, Bigger Problems

The Covid-19 pandemic is an effective weapon of mass distraction from big tech's bad behavior. No news story survives 12 hours while a pandemic coupled with a national display of incompetence renders everything else what it is, less important.

But whether we are paying attention or not, unchecked growth and market dominance lead to a slew of problems. Inevitably, companies without serious competition become less innovative and capture more profits and share from exploiting their position, and less from creating real value. And to protect that position, they perform infanticide on other innovators. At the height of its power in the 1980s and '90s, Microsoft was notorious for its suppression of outside innovation. The company's first line of defense was "FUD": spreading fear, uncertainty, and doubt about competitive products, such as by suggesting they hadn't been thoroughly tested with Microsoft products, or that the competitor wasn't well capitalized, or anything else an enterprising sales rep could think to say. Microsoft was also fond of "vaporware"—announcing a product or feature to compete with a competitor, even though no such product would ever be released. In at least one notorious case,

Microsoft created fake error messages that appeared when a user installed competitive software.[11]

For today's big tech, the stakes are higher, because their power and potential for exploitation delves deeper into our lives and society. In the '90s, Bill Gates could keep a rival spreadsheet program from gaining traction. Today, Mark Zuckerberg can affect the outcome of a presidential election. Facebook is not merely plundering the technology budgets of America's corporations, as Microsoft did, but our private lives and emotional wellbeing, and the health of our democracy.

As these companies achieve a scale greater than 1990s Microsoft, their heft and integration into our lives becomes a risk. In the early days of the pandemic lockdown, when grocery store shelves started emptying and Amazon deliveries skyrocketed, we realized we had a new cohort of firms too big to fail. When companies become "too big to fail," they realize taking outsized risk is the right strategy, as the upside is privatized and the downside socialized—they get bailed out. This asymmetry of risk led banks to deploy leverage that nearly took the global economy down. So the shareholder-driven strategy for big tech is to demonstrate reckless abandon concerning elections, teen depression, kids with measles, radicalization of young men, and job destruction, as there appears to be little downside.

Big tech's role in sowing dissent and radicalization has been so well documented, it has become normalized. New, more egregious examples of putting profits over people surface regularly. Literally days before I finished work on this book, BuzzFeed reported that Facebook had received 455 complaints about a militia group calling for people to "take up arms" in Kenosha, Wisconsin, in response to protests there over a police shooting. Yet despite this abundant warning—the complaints made up 66% of all such reports Facebook received that day—and four separate moderator reviews, Facebook let this clear incitement of violence remain on the site.[12] Then, when two protesters were shot and killed in Kenosha, allegedly by an armed militia member, memes and posts celebrating the shooter proliferated across Facebook. One fundraiser for the shooter was shared over 17,000 times.[13] This followed a week after the release of a report finding that Facebook "actively promotes" Holocaust denial content,[14] and Facebook's admission that it had permitted thousands of pages and groups supporting QAnon to flourish on the site, despite links to, as NBC News summarized it, "violent, criminal incidents, including a train hijacking, kidnappings, a police chase, and a murder."[15]

It seems big tech firms rarely if ever consider the implications of their product design and policy decisions. Or they do, and still knowingly sacrifice the wellbeing of the commonwealth for private profit. It's an institutional code not to recognize the externalities of scale that led to Cambridge Analytica and content on YouTube that radicalizes young men. Anyone who asks "Have we thought about if this happens?" or, more generally, gets in the way of the answer to the profound question, "How would we go from 10 to 200 million daily active users?" gets sent to the Island of Misfit Careers. The temptation to be worth more than the U.S. auto industry, to be the era's Steve Jobs, the guy or gal who gets invited to speak at Stanford Business School, and bask in the warmth of our nation's idolatry of wealth and innovators is difficult to resist.

## STANDING UP AGAINST THE FOUR

Pushing back against this growth is difficult—there is little that individuals or even companies can do when firms become this powerful. This is the role of government. But big tech has public opinion on their side, hundreds of lobbyists, and they move faster than regulators can keep up. **Laws written by the light of coal power don't work against digitized monopolies.** Traditional antitrust principles focus on consumer harm through the prism of prices. Low prices are good, high prices are bad. It's not a framework well suited to companies that don't charge consumers, like Google or Facebook, or that relentlessly lower prices, like Amazon (and Apple with Apple TV+), but that nonetheless limit competition and cause consumer harm in other ways besides high prices. Nor does the current mainstream antitrust framework account for the ability of these firms to consolidate markets and outcompete competitors through their unique access to billions in low-cost capital.

Similarly, our content regulatory traditions were developed in the time of print media and broadcast communications. The

First Amendment's protection of freedom of speech is a cornerstone of American democracy, but it has never been absolute. Slander, calls for violence, breaches of confidentiality, and government secrecy have always been limited, and commercial speech restricted. But the way we draw those lines was developed when books had to be printed and sold one at a time and electronic media went out over mass airwaves. Now, anyone can reach an audience of millions, and sophisticated actors can deliver millions of individually customized messages to cohorts biased in specific ways as to be highly susceptible to targeted persuasion. As has often been said, **freedom of speech isn't freedom of reach**. Highly sophisticated Custom Audience algorithms can do a lot of damage to the democratic process when false or misleading ads can be targeted only to specific susceptible voters, rather than a large audience able to evaluate and critique them publicly. Coming down the pike are deepfakes (realistic but fake videos that can make it appear someone did or said something) and other tools of fake news that will further tear at our national fabric.

The public and the media are showing signs of waking up to these threats, though the road ahead is steep and narrow. The House antitrust subcommittee made headlines this summer when it called the CEOs of the Four to testify in one of several public hearings. What many, including me, thought would be an empty gesture instead revealed that the subcommittee has been doing its homework, and a clear majority of its members are deadly serious about reining in big tech.

In his opening remarks, subcommittee chair Representative David Cicilline laid out a vision for digital antitrust, focusing on big tech's data and reach. The subcommittee wasn't looking for more information, but signaling and trialing the legislation and antitrust action they will likely catalyze.

Leading the charge was Representative Pramila Jayapal. Armed with the companies' internal documents, testimony from the subcommittee's investigation, and the fervor of the righteous, Jayapal gave no quarter. Politicians are sometimes overmatched in these hearings, but Rep. Jayapal demonstrated she was more than talented enough to have been in the opposite seat, testifying in front of Congress about the anticompetitive practices of her own firm—but instead she long ago decided to serve her country. Her very first question went to her own constituent, Jeff Bezos, whom she forced into a serious concession about Amazon's likely misuse of third-party seller data. Having dispensed with the richest man in the world, she turned her fire on number three, and bloodied Mark Zuckerberg with a barrage of questions, based largely on Zuck's own emails, revealing Facebook's blatant copying of competitive products.

It has been widely reported that the FTC is likely to bring an antitrust action against Google, and if Congress can garner the will to pass expanded antitrust regulation, more such actions against other big tech players could follow.

We should stop thinking of the breakup of big tech as *punishment* for doing something wrong, or that it means tech leaders are bad people. Managers do what they can to raise shareholder value, that's their job. And when you get big enough, stifling competition and exploiting your power is a great way to secure short-term gains for your shareholders, so that's what managers do. We break companies up to restore competition to markets, which is the gangster app for a growing economy that demands better behavior. As a result, there are more options from other players who must then . . . behave better.

Antitrust is just one tool in the government's kit for addressing the dangerous power of big tech. Because it nurtures competition, it has the potential to be the most comprehensive. But other regulatory regimes may be needed to control big tech's abuse of our private data and its relentless promotion of misinformation and divisiveness. That's trickier than it might seem, because regulatory schemes can have unintended consequences. Strict pollution and labor laws can drive production to foreign countries with minimal environmental or labor controls. Decades of success fighting wildfires leads to fuel buildups that trigger even more destructive infernos. One of the biggest risk areas is that regulatory regimes meant to rein in big companies end up benefiting them, because they are the only companies with the resources to develop internal compliance teams and systems.

The current regulatory regime concerning tech content (such as Facebook posts, tweets, and Google search results) is largely governed by what's known as Section 230. Section 230 protects online platforms from liability for content users post on the platform, a protection essential to the growth of the internet as a communications medium. But that protection extends to dangerous content. There have been a lot of calls lately to revise Section 230, but no singular vision has emerged on the best path forward.

A recent move by Congress to trim Section 230's protections illustrates the risks of inelegant regulatory change. Congress was concerned about the boom in advertisements for adult services on sites like Craigslist and Backpage.com, because many of these ads were in fact ads selling the victims of sex trafficking. So in 2018, Congress passed what's known as FOSTA-SESTA. The bill limited Section 230's protections where the content in question was from sex traffickers. Even while the law was being debated, there were vocal opponents, many in the tech community, who warned that it would simply drive sex trafficking back underground, making it harder to stop, while suppressing legitimate and valuable commerce and online communication. Leading tech companies were initially opposed, but after the draft legislation was tweaked to its liking, Facebook strongly endorsed the legislation, and it passed into law.

It has been, more or less, a failure. As predicted, sex work activists report being forced back onto the streets and into the shadows, making sex work more dangerous and unstable. And there is little evidence the change suppressed sex trafficking. The feds shut down Backpage.com *before* FOSTA-SESTA even passed, using perfectly functional existing laws against, wait for it, sex trafficking. The most telling flaw has been the legislation's effect on competition. It led to a bunch of smaller dating sites shutting down because they were afraid they were going to be liable for illegal conduct. But soon after the bill passed, Facebook (whose support had been essential to the legislation's enactment) launched its own dating platform.

## The Curse of Big Numbers

Every big tech firm must implicitly, or explicitly, assure investors there is a reasonable chance their stock will double in the next five years. Otherwise investors will buy Zoom, Lemonade, or another "disruptive" firm. As their market caps increase, big tech's appetite is becoming increasingly difficult to sate, similar to Brad Pitt being forced to feed off humans, as rats just can't satisfy his thirst. Remember that movie? Pale and a bad haircut . . .

And. Still. Dreamy.

Google and Facebook could seize the remaining revenues of the radio and print industries, and they'd still wake up hungry for more revenues within 24–36 months, based on investors' expectations. The Four need to add nearly a trillion dollars to their revenue over the next five years. This requires entering new markets—and coming for one other. You can't feed a city on rabbit meat. You have to go big-game hunting. Where will they find this game?

# 6 LARGEST U.S. SECTORS BY REVENUE
2020 IN BILLIONS

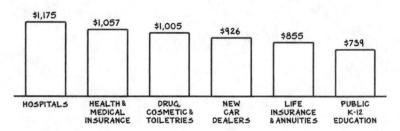

| HOSPITALS | HEALTH & MEDICAL INSURANCE | DRUG, COSMETIC & TOILETRIES | NEW CAR DEALERS | LIFE INSURANCE & ANNUITIES | PUBLIC K-12 EDUCATION |
|---|---|---|---|---|---|
| $1,175 | $1,057 | $1,005 | $926 | $855 | $739 |

SOURCE: IBIS WORLD.

# Amazon

Amazon's core competence is vision and storytelling. Bezos had the vision of selling everything online when that was unthinkable. An even bigger feat, Bezos and his team accomplished something unprecedented—they convinced investors not to expect short- or medium-term profits. While most firms' profits are reevaluated every three months on their quarterly earnings call, Bezos has retrained investors' Pavlovian mechanisms, replacing profits with vision and growth. Key to this decision was CFO Joy Covey, who recognized the best way to predict the future is to make it. And the best way to make the future is to gain access to cheap capital to pull the future forward with extraordinary investments others won't make, resulting in moats, which give you access to cheaper capital . . . and so on and so on. While most firms look for competitive advantage via lowest cost, Amazon looks for sustainable advantage that requires gargantuan investment.

The obvious beneficiary from the lockdown (the closure of retail and a fear of leaving the house) is—surprise!—the company that's in the business of bringing retail to your house. And though it gets less general media attention, Amazon is also a huge beneficiary of people spending more time online, thanks to Amazon's $40 billion Amazon Web Services division. Indeed, the federal government's $1,200 stimulus check program should have been called the Amazon Shareholder Support Act (ASSa). Not in their wildest dreams could Amazon shareholders devise this scenario: the government closes down the competition, restricts everyone to their homes, and then sends consumers trillions in cash. How do they not come out of this with so much momentum that competitors never catch up? Investors will ask themselves, why shouldn't I just buy Amazon?

The pandemic in a business nutshell:

- Stuck at home
- Netflix
- Hate my spouse
- Starting to hate my children
- Jeff Bezos gets his divorce paid for in 30 days

Mr. Bezos increased his wealth by approximately $35 billion in 30 days. In 2018, the tech and business press was aflutter with the question of who would be the first trillion-dollar company, Apple or Amazon. Apple won that race by a nose, and reached $2 trillion in August 2020. But there shouldn't be any doubt about who will be the first $3 trillion company. Everyone is going to throw in the towel, investors, the government, consumers, and go all in on Amazon. Amazon—first $3 trillion company by the end of 2023.

Between Prime, AWS, and the Marketplace, Amazon has the largest flywheel in the history of business. What are they going to do with it?

One of Amazon's arsenal of gangster moves is turning expense lines into revenue lines. It's one of Bezos's best tricks, and like so much else they do, it is made possible by a combination of scale and ultra-low-cost capital. This is how it works. First, a company gets really good at its essential, but non-core, business functions. Amazon is an online store, so it needs a great web back end, which means a superior data center. World-class data centers are essential to Amazon's business, but running them is not its core business. The way most companies get really good at stuff like this is they pay someone else to do it. That's what business gurus have preached for decades: focus on your "core competencies" and outsource everything else. Amazon flips this around. It doesn't pay someone else to run its data center. It takes advantage of its massive data center volume, and its ability to invest essentially unlimited capital, and the company builds the best data center management competency on the planet. That's step one.

Step two is Amazon turns around and starts selling that

competency to other companies as a service. Thus is born AWS, the largest cloud services provider by a wide margin. As firms whose roots are in technology and software, vs. retail, Microsoft and Google should own this market, and AWS does more business than the two combined. Amazon did the same thing with warehouse and distribution, first erecting the ability to deliver millions of products in 48 hours, then offering the service to other retailers through Amazon Marketplace. Now over 20% of Amazon's revenue comes from Marketplace. Payments used to be 2% of Amazon's costs, so they turned that into an R&D expense and spun out Amazon Payments.

## AMAZON TURNS COST CENTERS INTO REVENUE DRIVERS

| 2005 COST CENTERS | IN MILLIONS | 2020 REVENUE DRIVERS | | |
|---|---|---|---|---|
| NET SALES | $ 8,490 | | | |
| PRODUCT COST | 6,212 → | amazonbasics | amazon publishing | amazonstudios |
| SHIPPING COST | 239 | | | |
| GROSS PROFITS | $ 2,039 | | | |
| | | | | |
| OPERATING EXPENSES | | | | |
| FULFILLMENT | $ 522 → | amazon fulfillment | | |
| TECHNOLOGY & CONTENT | 406 → | aws | | |
| MARKETING | 192 → | amazon marketplace | amazonadvertising | |
| PAYMENT PROCESSING | 207 → | amazon pay | | |
| GENERAL & ADMINISTRATIVE | 146 → | amazon business | | |
| INCOME FROM OPERATIONS | $ 566 | | | |

SOURCE: SOCIAL CAPITAL.

Amazon generated $89 billion in revenue in Q2 2020, greater than the annual budget of the Department of Education

($68 billion), or enough to end malaria worldwide. So how do we know where Amazon will go next? Simple. What are its biggest expenses? The vision to see expenses as investments in future stand-alone businesses is Latin for "3 trillion."

In July 2017 we predicted,[16] "If Bezos tomorrow said, 'We see overnight delivery as a huge opportunity,' the $150 billion of market cap of DHL, FedEx, and UPS would begin leaking to Amazon." This has happened. Since the launch of Amazon's delivery service in February 2018, FedEx has lost $25 billion (39%) in value, despite the S&P's 24% gain. Amazon has added $240 billion (33%). In less than two years, Amazon captured nearly one-fifth of the market for ecommerce deliveries in the U.S.

Since 2014, U.S. ecommerce has increased 84%, creating a massive opportunity for the delivery industry. But instead, there has been a transfer of wealth from FedEx, UPS, and the U.S. government to Amazon. Amazon enters high-friction, low-margin businesses as a means of differentiating low-friction, high-margin businesses (AWS and AMG).

Amazon seized the pandemic opportunity. At the outset of the company's May 2020 earnings call, Jeff Bezos warned shareholders they "may want to take a seat." He has done this several times. "This" is snatching profits from the jaws of shareholders to reinvest in the firm. With the exception of Netflix, no firm has been given this much runway. Bezos has used every foot of it to set aloft a vessel that nobody will likely catch. Imagine a Spruce Goose but at twice the speed of sound.

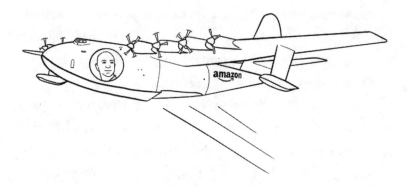

Bezos told investors that the $4 billion in profits they were expecting would be reinvested. The investment had a theme: Covid-19. Specifically, Bezos outlined a vision for at-home Covid tests, plasma donors, PPE equipment, distancing, additional compensation, and protocols to adapt to a new world.[17] Amazon is developing the earth's first "vaccinated" supply chain.

Great strategy cuts a swath between market conditions and a firm's assets. Put more simply, strategy is a firm's answer to the following question:

## WHAT CAN WE DO THAT IS REALLY HARD?

I believe Amazon will offer Prime members testing at a scale and efficiency that makes America feel like South Korea (competent). The "vaccinated" supply chain, as tested and safe as possible, will create a more muscular and immune fulfillment organism, offering stakeholders paramount value—real and perceived.

Leadership is the ability to convince people to work together in pursuit of a common goal. Bezos's decision to spend billions to ensure the safety of his supply chain stems from a vision that's obvious only after being crazy/genius.

The big payoff for Amazon is healthcare. Here too, the pandemic has accelerated the company's inevitable move into this space. One of Amazon's core skills is that it sits on a massive collection of data, and it uses that to pick off the profitable parts of a business and farm out the less attractive elements. There are a few places Amazon can go with healthcare. First is likely insurance. As we saw with Lemonade's spectacular IPO in July 2020, there is a disruption opportunity in the insurance field. Consumers by and large dislike and distrust insurance companies, and for good reason. It's a bloated industry, protected by inefficient state regulatory schemes and entrenched relationships. That's fat and slow prey for the business world's apex predator.

Amazon knows a great deal about its best customers: what do they eat, do they buy exercise equipment or video games, do they have children, and are they in a relationship. Between Amazon and Whole Foods purchases, the Amazon card, and all the "pay with Amazon" merchants, the company has vastly more individualized data than any insurance actuary. And with more and more people working in the gig economy or as long-term freelancers, more and more people are responsible for their own health insurance. If you are one of them, don't be surprised to hear your Alexa ask, "Are you interested in saving 25% on your health insurance?" CFOs can expect a call from a Bezos lieutenant offering the same deal across their employee base.

But that's just the beginning. Amazon is well positioned to address the financial cost of healthcare, and better positioned to reduce the non-financial costs—time, effort, and anxiety. Your son has a rash, and you ask Alexa to connect you with a dermatologist, who asks you to hold up his arm to the intelligent camera. The dermatologist is likely not an Amazon employee, because that part of the business doesn't scale. Instead she pays a percentage of her revenues to "Prime Health," what I think Amazon might call the most robust, liquid remote healthcare platform on the planet.

A depth of specialists and reviews sitting beneath the second most-used search engine helps Prime Health members get to just the right physician, right now, at lower cost. The platform is fully integrated with the retail platform, resulting in a more "holistic" approach to healthcare. You don't have to do anything but log on, and the Prime dermatologist has instant access to your kid's medical records, as the Seattle firm has invested the necessary capital to make its systems HIPAA compliant. Prime Health would also have a 3-D scan of his body and recent readings of his vital signs through Halo, Amazon's fitness wearable announced August 2020.[18] A prescription is sent to Amazon-owned pharmacy PillPack, which delivers the steroid cream by Amazon Fulfillment, and (in the largest metros) it arrives within the hour. If the doctor wants a blood test, a home test kit is in the package as well, or a urine jar, a DNA swab (but why not just make that part of the Prime Health onboarding?), or a hundred other diagnostic devices that Amazon has invested billions to develop. The source of this firepower (cheap capital) will arrive on the day they announce a healthcare service, and the stock increases over $100 billion that trading day.

None of this is new, at least in the minds of futurists and science fiction writers. But the barriers of capital cost, regulation, and entrenched special interest have been immovable objects. The pandemic swept them aside in weeks. In spring 2020, doctors across the country were seeing patients in online sessions and being reimbursed by Medicare and private insurance companies—something that had required onerous special licensing requirements just weeks earlier. Doctors have seen firsthand the benefits for their patients: fewer cancelled appointments and increased efficiency. And of course, no capital investment is out of reach for big tech.

# Apple

By achieving a business paradox—a low-cost product that sells for a premium price—Apple became the most profitable company in history in 2014. Leaping from the tech sector (low margins, zero sex appeal) to the luxury sector (the volumes of Toyota with the irrational margins of Ferrari), Apple owns the

most profitable product ever made, the iPhone, and sells it
through the highest per-square-foot retail business of all time,
the Apple Store.

Yet even just a few years ago, a pandemic would have put
Apple's status as a member of the Four at serious risk. Apple
has always been unique in the group, as it manufactures and
sells physical objects for profit. A slowdown in employment
and worries about economic prospects force greater scrutiny
on every purchase. However, firms that ask the consumer to
make one decision a year, or until you decide to opt out or cancel, are much more resilient, as it is often a bundle, increasing
the exit costs across fewer decisions. In addition, the ability to
ask the consumer to enter into a monogamous relationship (a
subscription) requires a choice that is more of an IQ test than a
decision. The recurring revenue bundles that get attraction are
forced to be incredible value propositions from the outset. Recurring revenue bundles are expensive, hard, and enduring.

As Apple ran up against the law of big numbers, the firm
invested heavily in recurring revenue offerings—iCloud, Apple
Music, Apple TV+, Arcade, etc. In Q4 2019, Apple's services revenue was up 25% year over year to 23% of revenue. As a result,
Apple has been recast as a software firm, and despite a negli-
gible increase in earnings, it doubled its valuation and P/E multiple in just 12 months. Apple's services business would stand
as the 258th company on the Fortune 500, just beating out
Bed Bath & Beyond.[19] And on the hardware side, the company
is transitioning one-off sales of its flagship iPhone into a monthly

service through the iPhone Upgrade Program. Tim Cook said he believed that model would "grow disproportionately."[20]

We are likely entering into the mother of overdue global slowdowns. Every executive team needs to explore the limits of their comfort zone and imagine a business with 20% less revenue, that commands twice the value. There is only one path to a dramatic increase in stakeholder value in the face of flat/declining revenues: The *rundle*—my term for "a recurring revenue bundle."

This was a strategic move before the pandemic—now it's gangster. That revenue is substantially immune to short-term pandemic disruptions and can cover for softness in the core hardware businesses.

The other big save that Cook and Company have made in recent years is how successfully Apple has disarticulated itself from the rest of big tech. In large part, this is due to their business model, which is blue/iOS. And Cook pushed that divide wide open in 2018 with one of the most devastating CEO interviews in history. When my *Pivot* cohost, Kara Swisher, asked him, in the wake of Facebook's serial privacy scandals, "What would you do if you were Mark Zuckerberg?" Tim Cook fired back, "I wouldn't be in this situation." Apple, he pointed out, had chosen not to turn its customers into products for data mining. "Privacy to us is a human right." Facebook, you're no Jack Kennedy, and you're fundamentally fucked up.

Cook can seize the high ground here due to his company's

business model, and because Apple remains one of the last of the great brand builders. Apple doesn't need broadcast media anymore, with stores and "earned" media. However, the world's strongest consumer brand will always be a multichannel marketer, and it recognizes that the assault on broadcast media has brought costs down such that they (again) make sense for building intangible associations (brand).

The pandemic test for Apple will be in the supply chain—can they get new products to consumers? Most likely yes. China, South Korea, and other Asian countries' competent response to the pandemic looks to have barely dented what is likely the world's second most robust supply chain, Amazon.

## THINK RUNDLE

Where does Apple go from here? Double down on the recurring revenue that has powered it through the pandemic. The only thing better than recurring revenue is a recurring revenue bundle that could form a flywheel. Why not one with a literal flywheel?

Peloton riders are fanatics. The wildly popular Official Peloton Member Facebook page has over 330,000 members. This cohort posts 23 times an hour and interacts with high engagement. Just as The League introduces Ivy League socialites to each other, JDate connects Jewish singles, and Raya connects models and the social elite, Peloton could begin connecting fitness-minded singles who become more engaged, riding and swiping.

I believe there is a floor on Peloton stock, as there are few firms that are a more obvious/natural acquisition by Apple than Peloton. Apple could pay a 50% premium for all the outstanding stock of the Apple of fitness and register less than a 2% dilution. The acquisition of Peloton would provide the world's most valuable firm with an additional, if more cumbersome, wearable that has greater margins than the most profitable product in history, the iPhone. The tie-up would also take Apple from letter $D$ to $G$ in one of only two sectors that can move the needle on a $2 trillion firm—healthcare. (The other is education.)

In 2018, estimates were Apple TV+ would spend $1 billion on original content for the envisioned streaming video offering. But in August 2019, they announced $6 billion for original content. So, a tech hardware firm is devoting the same capital to content featuring Reese Witherspoon and Khal Drogo (Jason Momoa) as the state of California allocates to the 23-campus California State University system.[21] If it sounds as if we're living in a dystopia, trust your instincts.

Thanks to Tim Cook's newfound love for Hollywood, Apple TV+ is distinguished by all-original content at $4.99 a month. For every $1 that you spend a month, the company spends $1 billion on content a year (about the same as Netflix). The quality of their offerings does not rival HBO's, but the world's premier brand builders know better than to clutter up their original content with *The Big Bang Theory*. Apple continues to be the benchmark of brand management.

As a result, Apple is also in a position to offer a Prime-like rundle. Just send me the latest iWhatever with unlimited media (television, games, apps) activated on the good phone at $50 a month, $100 for the better phone plus watch, and $150 for online classes on design and UX/UI and an iPeloton. Amazon is still going to beat Apple to being the first $3 trillion company, but if Apple goes full rundle, they won't be far behind.

## Mad Men 2.0: Google and Facebook

Two of the Four are in the advertising business, and traditionally advertising is a lousy business when the economy goes south. This time is different, because even though we are seeing a dip in ad spend, the timing is such that it will rebound to Google and Facebook's benefit. They can survive the downturn. Many of their traditional media competitors, already on the ropes from two decades of being on the wrong end of a duopoly, won't. Covid-19 has a mortality rate of around 0.5–1% among people, but the pandemic is going to have a fatality rate of 10–20% in traditional media.

This is a function of weak balance sheets and investors who have lost patience—the same culling we can expect in most industries. Also, being trapped at home increases inventory for Facebook and Google advertisers. Yes, you are "inventory."

Beyond that, traditional media faces another challenge: the pandemic is highlighting their truth. Facebook and Google are simply more effective platforms for advertisers, and the truth will become increasingly apparent as even the biggest advertisers start cutting spend on traditional media. They won't miss it. No other platform can offer the combination of scale and granularity that Facebook and Google provide. They are the most effective advertising vehicles in history and, at 8 million advertisers, Facebook has the most elastic, self-healing customer base in business history.

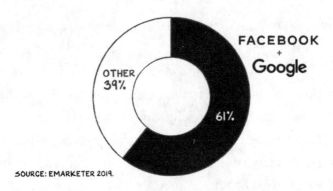

## SHARE OF DIGITAL AD SPENDING
2020

OTHER 39%

FACEBOOK + Google

61%

SOURCE: EMARKETER 2019.

Advertisers also won't miss traditional media, since the thing traditional media advertising does best—build mass brands—is increasingly irrelevant as we graduate from the Brand Age to the Product Age. There is a double bind here, because brand equity erodes slowly, and a few months of reduced spend isn't going to move any needles. Which will make it that much harder even for marketers still attending the church of brand equity to justify returning their traditional media spend to pre-pandemic levels.

The other benefit for Facebook and Google is the distraction. Pre pandemic, these two firms were in the news cycle more often, for all the wrong reasons. From ISIS recruitment videos and pedophiles on YouTube to Russian operatives and data thieves on Facebook, the drumbeats for a regulatory response were building.

Then the pandemic happened. And as long as testing, masks, and infection rates continue to dominate the news cycle, they will dominate politics, and Google and Facebook get a reprieve from public scrutiny. However, the business model remains intact, benefiting from conspiracy theory content the pandemic has spurred. Both firms have made an effort to limit misinformation about Covid, but the rage and alienation that powers their endless feeds continues unabated.

Summer 2020 saw a feeble attempt by well-meaning advertisers to push back against Facebook, but it was predictably over before it started. Around one thousand advertisers publicly pulled their ad spending on Facebook in July, joining a campaign organized by civil rights groups in protest of Facebook's continued promotion of hate speech and misinformation. Also some major advertisers, such as Walmart and Procter & Gamble, cut or eliminated their July spending without making any public statement. The difference in spend was measurable but meaningless—the company still grew its year-over-year ad revenue by 10% in the first three weeks of July. Zuck scoffed at the threat on the firm's July 30 earnings call, saying that "some seem to wrongly assume that our business is dependent on a few large advertisers." Indeed, Facebook has over 7 million customers, and the top 100 account for only 16% of its revenue.[22] Meanwhile, the boycott may have backfired on the advertisers. Not only did they lose the business their Facebook ads would have brought in, but their absence created a void for counterfeiters and scammers to fill—because Facebook ads work on an auction model, reduced spend means reduced prices. Analyst Matt Stoller reported on a luxury shoe company that participated in the boycott, only to see ads for counterfeit versions of their shoes pop up where their own ads would normally have run.[23] With 8 million advertisers, and a model that creates immediate opportunity for others when one reduces spend, Facebook possesses the most robust (self-healing, even) customer base in the history of business.

By virtue of being the biggest elephants in the herd, the Four are well positioned to survive any crisis, and to thrive when the rains return. And a pandemic that keeps us home in front of our screens and leaves the professional class with plenty of unspent income is hardly a crisis at all for the companies that sell us those screens and dominate what we do on them. The Four were already ascending to dominance, and the pandemic has accelerated that trend, just as it has so many others.

# OTHER DISRUPTORS

## The Disruptability Index

The Four have made the jump to light speed and enjoy monopoly/duopoly power that results in hegemony of distribution, cemented by cheap capital, rendering them difficult to challenge. However, it's a big global economy, and there are other industries sticking their chins out. Again, the pandemic is accelerating these opportunities, making chins bigger and fists of stone fleeter.

The opportunity for disruption in an industry can be correlated to a handful of factors—a disruptability index. The key signal is dramatic increase in price with no accompanying increase in value or innovation. This is also known as *unearned margin*. The poster child for this is my sector, higher education. Consider a university lecture. Whether you are 19 or 90, you likely picture the same thing. An auditorium, an older person at the front, a group of young people in the seats, lecture, notes, teaching assistants. Almost nothing has changed in forty years, or even eighty. But there has been one dramatic change—the price. College tuition has increased 1,400% in the past 40 years.[1] A red flag for disruption.

Another industry ripe for disruption: healthcare. It's true that healthcare can claim significant quality improvements in certain sectors—advanced procedures, drug treatments, devices. But many outcomes, like life expectancy and infant mortality, have not improved dramatically. The consumer experience has not improved for most of us. Meanwhile, costs have exploded. The average premium for family coverage has increased 22% over the last five years and 54% over the last ten years, significantly more than wages or inflation.[2]

Another factor of disruptability is a reliance on brand equity divorced from the quality of the product, its distribution, or support. The transition from the Brand Age to the Product Age will erode the competitive advantage once possessed by many of the dominant firms of the twentieth century. Many companies sell essentially the same mass produced, mediocre product, but registered a premium due to a multigenerational investment in brand building. Digital technologies unleashed a torrent of innovation that brought differentiation, or not, to almost every consumer category. The temptation to ignore start-ups with bet-

ter materials/ingredients, mastery of new platforms, distribution, or communities, and to default to brand building is best
reflected in the near-irrelevance of the Masters of Yesterday—
communications holding companies.

## MARKET CAP ADDED SINCE APRIL 2020 VS. TOTAL MARKET CAP OF TRADITIONAL MEDIA FIRMS

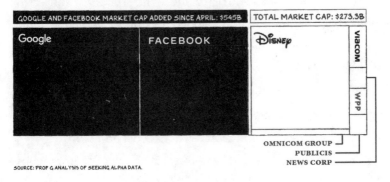

SOURCE: PROF G ANALYSIS OF SEEKING ALPHA DATA.

The chaser here is a reservoir of consumer ill will. Many
firms and industries have fostered an adversarial relationship
with consumers. Insurance comes by this naturally, as the business model consists of charging a consumer indefinitely and
deploying resources to avoid ever delivering the benefit. Despite its noble mission and the talent the sector attracts, healthcare also suffers from a bitter aftertaste. Much of this is because
our experience with healthcare is mediated through insurance
firms and regulation, which create obstacles between need and
care. Much of the industry centers its operations on the insurance payer and the doctor/institution provider. Disruptive
health clinics, including One Medical and ZOOM+Care, and

online pharmacy Capsule, are centering on the consumer/ patient.

Industries become ripe for disruption when existing players fail to adopt technological change to improve quality and value, as it may threaten their core business. A decent signal an industry is vulnerable is the presence of pseudo innovation—the addition of features that add no real value to the product; membership clubs that don't deliver any real savings or convenience; movie theaters whose online ordering is more of a hassle than buying the ticket at the venue; colleges investing in luxury accommodations instead of educational resources. Those are the home remedies of a management team that knows the patient requires surgery but doesn't want to endure real cost and pain.

The pandemic has laid bare the soft tissue of sectors whose major innovation has been price increases. The weaknesses of the U.S. healthcare system are a national tragedy. Among the myriad shortcomings, our reliance on centralized facilities, emergency room services in particular, might catalyze a tsunami of innovation around remote medicine and telehealth.

To survive, companies have scaled different dimensions of their business up or down with incredible agility. If a restaurant did a small amount of takeout, they've made it a priority, adjusting the menu, layout, and hours. In many places, third-party delivery services, including Seamless and Postmates, filled the need, took custody of the customer relationship, and now they have restaurants by the throat.

If your company was already adept at click and collect, as

Home Depot was, the pandemic is more a speed bump than a meteor. If your store was not ecommerce competent (T.J.Maxx, Marshalls), you've suffered, as the world a decade from now (i.e., now) is unforgiving of sub-par direct-to-consumer offerings.

## The Burning of the Unicorn Barn

Today's tech "start-ups" are more often well capitalized, professionally staffed operations, with access to enough capital that, with some market receptivity, can become formidable forces in their sectors in months, compared to what used to take years or even decades. Until very recently they were typically headed by a charismatic founder, long on vision, shadowed by an operator.

There is always a tension between capital and management. However, it appears we have reached peak founder worship, a transition that is being accelerated by the pandemic. In the 1990s on Sand Hill Road, founder-CEOs at tech start-ups were considered necessary evils—crazy, eccentric young white men with a vision who would eventually be sidelined as an older, more experienced executive would be brought in to scale the firm.

The power resided with capital—with the slightly older, much less eccentric white men on Sand Hill Road. And it was verboten for a founder to cash out of a company before the VCs managed to get their own liquidity. Founders' equity was dead equity until an acquisition or IPO.

I tried bucking the rules and did a secondary offering at one of my early companies, Red Envelope—I sold a million dollars of my own stock to an outside investor. Within 24 months, the company was going sideways, and I was forced to reinvest that full million dollars or be washed out by my lead VC, Sequoia Capital.

However, in the late 1990s and early 2000s the power began to swing back toward founders. Entrepreneurs started to be seen as the secret sauce within companies. Why? Two reasons: Bill Gates and Steve Jobs. Bill Gates was the first to prove the same person could found a company and take it to $100 billion in value. Gates grew Microsoft to $600 billion over 14 years.

Jobs built Apple to $600 million in value over the company's first five years. But that was then, and he was forced out in 1985 on the basis of being eccentric, stubborn, and mercurial. There are few things that indicate an information age jerk more than a CEO wearing a black turtleneck and telling people to find their passion. However, Jobs was in fact a genius, and none of the gray hairs that followed—Scully, Spindler, or Emilio—could grow the company. Twenty years after Jobs returned to Apple, the firm had increased in value by 200 times.

With those proof points, founders became more assertive. And as the tech boom roared on, supply and demand shifted in their favor. In 1985, the Valley was full of geniuses with world-changing ideas, but capital was hard to come by. In 2005, we weren't making *that* many more true geniuses, but available capital began to increase exponentially. VCs jockeying to fund successful founders devised term sheets that included secondary sales, two-class shareholder structures, and other founder-friendly terms.

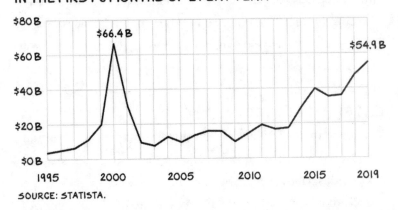

# U.S. VENTURE CAPITAL FUNDING
## IN THE FIRST 6 MONTHS OF EVERY YEAR

SOURCE: STATISTA.

The situation would only get more out of balance. The NASDAQ quadrupled in ten years, everybody wanted in on the boom, but the pool of talent has not kept pace. Markets abhor a vacuum, and this one was filled by fake prophets, who've managed to coax a flock into thinking they are the next Jesus Christ of our economy—the next Steve Jobs.

Two other factors pushed the founder-worship era to greater heights. The sheer amount of capital meant that companies could pursue capital-driven growth strategies. That is, they could buy market share by selling at a loss, while raising subsequent rounds of capital, at increasing valuations, due to growth that was fueled by cheap capital. And with all this private capital available, companies could stay on this money-losing merry-go-round longer before going public (and subjecting itself to the scrutiny of the public markets). The number of U.S. IPOs has declined 88% from 1996 to 2016. It also takes much longer for companies to get public. The average age of a company up for IPO increased from three to eight years over the last 20 years. The two dynamics fed on one another, and "visionary" founders feasted. A new species of start-up emerged: the unicorn.

## ENTER THE UNICORN

Way back in 2013, when billion-dollar start-ups were actually rare beasts, venture capitalist Aileen Lee coined the term *unicorn* to describe them.[3] She found 39 such companies and reported that new ones came along at a rate of about 4 per year. Estimates put the number today at around 400, with 42 born in 2019 alone.

Not every unicorn runs on hype, though several bought into the philosophy of "fake it till you make it" and achieved only one of those things. From criminality (Theranos) to consensual hallucination (WeWork) to just overvalued businesses (Casper), these are companies that relied on a combination of sycophantic business media, FOMO-infected investors, and cynical faith that multiple rounds with stepped-up valuations would create enough momentum to carry the firm through a sale of their shares to a greater fool.

It's always going to be "different this time." People love WeWork and Uber as I loved Pets.com and Urban Fetch. A 60-pound bag of dog food and a pint of Ben & Jerry's delivered the next day or hour for less than cost was awesome, except for shareholders. Value is a function of growth and margins. As they did in the '90s, many of today's unicorns have deployed massive capital to achieve the former while not demonstrating the value proposition to achieve the latter.

The pandemic finds the start-up world at a unique juncture. Never before has there been so much capital and so many built-out, well-positioned companies, just as the mother of all accelerants is creating disruption opportunities left and right. The difference this time is that most unicorns will survive in one form or another, but the value destruction may be greater, as the valuations have become so extraordinary.

## SOFTBANK'S $100 BILLION UNICORN BUFFET

Foremost among the suppliers of cheap capital has been SoftBank, whose $100 billion Vision Fund was disruptive on several levels. The case study we'll be teaching for decades in B-schools around the world about the Vision I disaster writes itself. The strategy was (wait for it) capital as a strategy. Specifically, more of it, so you could win deal flow and be the fuel that helps portfolio firms make the jump to light speed, leaving competitors behind and befuddled. The pitch from SoftBank to entrepreneurs was simple and compelling. "You aren't thinking big enough. We want to invest three times your planned raise, and if you don't do a deal with us, we'll inject these liters of growth hormone capital into your biggest competitor." Well, okay then.

Capital is in fact a weapon in private equity, where only a few firms can bid for the truly great, proven assets with enormous cash flows. However, in venture, and growth, the secret sauce is dislocation, a market ripe for disruption, and crazy genius founders who are too stupid to know they will fail. When your ability to deploy billions into a concept becomes the priority, as it does when you have $100 billion to deploy, your returns go down. This is evident across SoftBank's portfolio.

My NYU colleague Professor Pankaj Ghemawat published gangster research showing business and trade are, despite rumors of the death of distance, a function of geography. A retail store's profitability is correlated with proximity to HQ. Sequoia Capital was the lead investor in my second firm, and the partner on our board told me a key tenet was they would not invest in a firm the partner could not drive to. Note: as they've raised bigger funds, tier-1 VCs make investments all over the world but often open local offices.

Masayoshi Son and Adam Neumann would agree to meet in-between their 13 time zones (I think that's Hawaii). Similar to when the Japanese acquired U.S. movie studios and golf courses in the 1980s, SoftBank will leave with fewer yen than it came with. If you found the previous sentence uncomfortable, racist even (as I initially did), you've fallen victim to the same monoculture PC virus infecting our universities. Japan did buy U.S. golf courses, and their currency is in fact the yen.

## ROI VS. DISTANCE FROM MASA

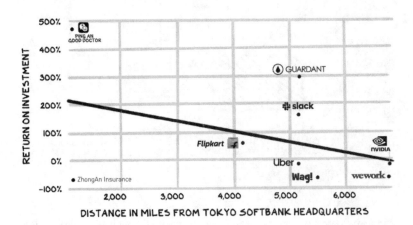

SOURCE: SECTION4.

Another tenet of venture, expressed by every investor I've raised money from (General Catalyst, Maveron, Sequoia, Weston Presidio, JPMorgan, Goldman Sachs, and others), is **they do not like to lead subsequent rounds**. Good investors resist the temptation to "smoke their own supply" (lead multiple rounds) and require third-party, arms-distance validation of the firm's value here and now. SoftBank was the only lead investor in WeWork, through multiple rounds, since 2016.

Ironically, the real damage on the capital side will be on SoftBank employees, as they own common stock in Vision I. Saudi Arabia Public Investment Fund and Mubadala own preferred stock that captures a 7% (preferred) return each year,

## LEAD INVESTOR VS. ROI
N = 9 COMPANIES

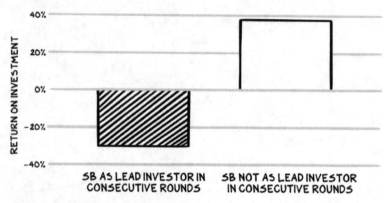

SOURCE: SECTION4.

siphoning returns from the few winners in the portfolio. So, Vision I has pneumonia, but the common equity holders in Vision I are on a ventilator.

The availability of capital is not correlated with the availability of good places to invest the capital. Good investments—disruptive start-ups with the potential to grow into sustainable multibillion-dollar enterprises—will always be scarce. The alchemy of crazy brilliant entrepreneurs who have unique visions of how new technologies can solve problems or make our lives better, coupled with fat and happy incumbents, is a story of hunting for unicorns. But capital is wealth in motion, and like the sharks that deploy it, it has to stay in motion—or it dies. So, when good companies seem to have retreated to the forest, capital will convince itself that a bear is a unicorn.

## YOGABABBLE

Too much capital and not enough talent is the cue for the rise of the charismatic founder. All things being equal, a charismatic founder is an asset. They not only attract capital, they attract great employees, sell the product, and provide a halo for the company when it faces threats. But in a capital-soaked environment, nobody has time or interest in the serious analysis of financial statements or diligence on a start-up's idea. It's easier to invest hundreds of millions with the guy with long hair who has a plan to live forever and (presumably sooner) solve the Israeli-Palestinian conflict, as he's a "visionary," and we (capital) "back people, not companies."

The charismatic founder speaks in a characteristic dialect: **yogababble**. That's our term for abstract or spiritual-sounding language in IPO's S-1s, a company's formal disclosure before going public. Besides listing the required financial disclosures, the company amplifies the yogababble with the power of the corporate communications executive. This is an affliction at real companies (according to LinkedIn, there are more corporate comms personnel working for Bezos at Amazon (969) than journalists working for Bezos at *The Washington Post* (798)), but it becomes a core competency at the charismatic-founder, capital-driven growth company. When firms are still searching for a viable business model, the temptation to go full yogababble gets stronger, as the truth (numbers, business model, EBITDA) needs concealer. When I show up at MSNBC, they put some crazy foundation syrup in a plastic bottle attached to a hose, ask everyone to stand back, and (no joke) spray my face and head as if the makeup artist were the last line of defense against the reactor 4 at Chernobyl. And I look awesome . . . for a while. But similar to yogababble, the concealer wears off.

Yogababble basically translates to "We are fascinating people," rather than "This is a solid company that makes sense for the following reasons."

We recently looked at the S-1 language of a bunch of tech firms and made a qualitative assessment of the level of bullshit—their willingness to depart from the fundamentals of balance sheets and flee into the realm of the mysterious. Their attempt to captivate by dimming the lights, as it were. Then we looked at their performance one year post IPO—what happens when the lights come on. We believe there is an inverse correlation between the two, and that may be a forward-looking indicator for a firm's share performance.

**Yogababble scale 1–10:**

1/10: I'm a professor of marketing who likes dogs.

5/10: I'm the Big Dawg.

10/10: I am a Spirit Dawg that unlocks self-actualization.

### Zoom

**Mission:** "To make video communications frictionless."

*This is accurate. Zoom is a video communications company. It offers less friction, as demonstrated by a higher NPS score (62) than Webex (6).*

**Bullshit rating**: 1/10

**Stock return 6 months post IPO:** +122%

### Spotify

**Mission**: "To unlock the potential of human creativity by giving a million creative artists the opportunity to live off their art and billions of fans the opportunity to enjoy and be inspired by these creators."

*OK, sort of. But hard to see how Celine Dion is unlocking human creativity.*

**Bullshit rating**: 5/10

**Stock return 1 year post IPO:** +9%

### Peloton

**Mission**: "On the most basic level, Peloton sells happiness."

*Nope, similar to Chuck Norris, Christie Brinkley, and Tony Little, you sell exercise equipment.*

**Bullshit Rating**: 9/10

**Stock return 1 day post IPO:** –11%. Granted, after being mostly even for the first 6 months since its IPO, Peloton has shot up during the pandemic as people move to working out from home.

I can relate to the mix of hubris, success, and Christ complex that leads you to believe your business efforts deserve a vision worthy of your genius—if not to distract you and your investors from the reality of how hard it is to build an entity that takes in more money than it spends, while growing. When the board, CEO, and bankers transfer the vicious hangover to retail investors, the distraction becomes malfeasance.

My new firm, Section4, was going to "Restore the Middle Class." My colleagues rolled their eyes so hard I wondered if they'd been coached by my twelve-year-old son. Then we were "NSFW Business Media" or "Streaming MBA." We're trying to figure it out. Eventually, I told the board we had assembled a group of talented people, and will deliver elite business school marketing and strategy electives for 10% of the price. We'll go from there. I've come to the realization that we're not bringing joy to the universe. We are not Chipotle.

## THOROUGHBRED VS. UNICORN

As we enter the last quarter of 2020, VCs are raising record funds and valuations appear to be ripping higher after a brief (hot-minute) pause during the first half of 2020. But while funding has survived and even accelerated, I believe there will be an enduring impact on valuations. Firms cast as innovators have registered valuations that will be unsustainable when the markets realize. Fine print on my predictions, however: in March 2019, in front of a large audience at SXSW, I predicted Tesla's stock would decline from $300 to less than $100. It began 2020 at $430, and by August, surpassed $2,000 per share. In any event, it's possible the market will continue to overvalue recent IPOs, but to me many of these companies have valuations that don't make sense.

A company can be a good business with solid prospects valued at $200 million, and an embarrassment to the markets valued at $1.1 billion. Casper went public in February 2020. Casper is a nice brand in a growing market—the sleep economy. Sure, call it that. The incumbents, mattress stores, are the stuff of Tarantino movies: you expect a guy with a sawed-off shotgun to roll in and take hostages. One of the key factors in a company's success isn't the company itself but the incompetence of the incumbents. It appears that hundreds of people were stirred from their slumber with the same vision. There are 175 online mattress retailers besides Casper. (Think about that.)

Casper's numbers illuminate signals of a frothy economy: firms that should be sold in the private market doing a kabuki dance ("technology" mentioned over 100 times in a prospectus), asking people to suspend their disbelief until the founders, VCs, and bankers sell their shares and get their fees. Here too, yogababble plays a starring role: "We believe we are the first company that understands and serves the Sleep Economy in a holistic way."

However, when reviewing the financials, it doesn't feel holistic or especially relaxing. On a per-mattress basis, Casper captures $1,362 in revenue. But it spends $761 on the mattress, $480 on sales and marketing, and an impressive $470 on administrative overhead. That's a loss of $349 per mattress. Does

## CASPER: PROFIT/LOSS PER MATTRESS

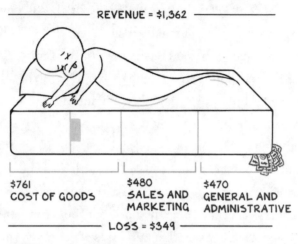

——— REVENUE = $1,362 ———

$761
COST OF GOODS

$480
SALES AND
MARKETING

$470
GENERAL AND
ADMINISTRATIVE

——— LOSS = $349 ———

SOURCE: ANALYSIS OF COMPANY FILINGS.

that sound like a billion-dollar business? It did to its venture backers, who bid it up to $1.1 billion in 2019.

I said Casper shouldn't go public and that if it did, the stock would shed 30%+ in the first year. In fact, I told the management team to sell in 2017. My advice was to sell to a retailer, like Target (one of their investors) or any middle-aged retailer looking for Botox, as Jet was to Walmart. The acquisition would provide the acquirer momentum in the sleep category, domain expertise in direct to consumer, and Casper would have a better chance of achieving the scale they don't have and need. Did they listen to the Dawg? They did not. Casper went public in February 2020, squeezing out the door at a valuation below their most recent funding as a private company, $1.1 billion—and fell 30% in the first week of trading—where it sits as I write this in August 2020.

To be fair, Casper saw an opportunity (so did the other 175 online mattress retailers) and pursued it with a combination of tech and narrative (mostly narrative). But it has struggled to develop any real differentiation, instead reverting to the Brand Age, and trying to wrap an undifferentiated product with aspirational associations.

## When the Smoke Clears

So, what does the start-up environment look like for would-be disruptors that can offer more than a dreamy founder with a good rap? Abundant capital remains, and the life cycle of a start-up has become a closed loop for a lot of companies.

Private investors—traditional venture capitalists, but also institutional investors whose appetite for risk has increased with their assets under management—are signing up for more and larger financing rounds, and using the public markets as an exit, instead of as a financing event.

Abundant capital permits a heft of financing rounds previously only available in the public markets, and a robust secondary market provides liquidity to shareholders. A major reason we are seeing so many unicorns is companies stay private longer. This has the benefit of reduced overhead and regulatory compliance costs, as well as less scrutiny. The company captures more of the upside for its private-market backers.

Another change has been the increased potential for another

form of high-return exit—acquisition by one of the mega tech companies like the Four. Also, ten or twenty years ago, exit by acquisition was typically a consolation prize for a venture-backed company. It could certainly make the founders money, but the real cabbage and fame was in an IPO. Now, just as the private capital markets can match the public markets, big acquirers can as well.

Apple has cash worth 200 unicorns ($200 billion) on its balance sheet. Google has $120 billion. But it's not just that the Four *can* pay IPO valuations—their dominance of markets (and ability to move aggressively into new ones) makes their offers difficult to refuse. The July 2020 congressional antitrust hearings revealed that Mark Zuckerberg had made Instagram an offer they couldn't refuse ("join or die"). The founders and investors typically do well in an acquisition. The 12 unicorns that exited in the first half of 2020 did so at a 91% premium to their last private valuation.[4] However, it's bad for the economy and job growth, as the ecosystem is less robust and the consolidation of the market makes it increasingly difficult for start-ups to get out of the crib.

The pandemic may birth the best-performing IPO class in several years, as the market's valuations are based on a firm's perceived performance 10 years ahead. The same is true of the downside: as firms that are struggling are issued a do-not-resuscitate order from the markets and are valued at their (remaining) cash flows. The cheap capital economy that offers disruptors the opportunity to pull the future forward sucks oxygen from the incumbents, who are forced to retrench (lay-off, cuts in CapEx) as the new kids on the block can lean into new investments and hiring. It becomes a self-fulfilling prophecy—incumbents are forced to play defense in order to maintain profits their investors have become addicted to. This further weakens the incumbents, giving the disruptors more momentum as market share gains become easier with sector elders weakened.

So what's the recipe of disruption? First, the industry you are entering is the crucial context. Sectors that have raised prices faster than inflation, without an equivalent increase in innovation, are the sectors where disruption is more likely. The DNA of a disruptor can be mapped via the disarticulation of key attributes of firms that have added hundreds of billions in stakeholder value in years vs. decades.

The T Algorithm, which I developed in *The Four*, and have refined since, defines some of these key qualities. The *T* stands for "trillion"—these are the traits that give a company a chance at a trillion-dollar valuation. The eight elements of the T Algorithm are as follows:

- Appealing to human instinct
- Accelerant
- Balancing growth and margins
- Rundle
- Vertical integration
- Benjamin Button products

- Visionary storytelling
- Likability

# T ALGORITHM

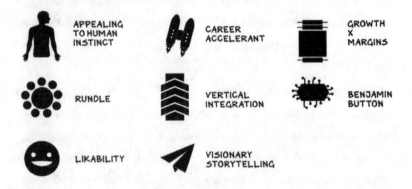

**Appealing to human instinct.** As humans, we are hardwired to share a set of biological needs. The most powerful firms have found ways to serve and exploit these instincts. We can break them down into four main categories, going down the torso. First, *the brain instinct*: we are constantly looking for answers to help explain our experiences and the world around us (Google). Bargains (Walmart) and rational claims (Dell, Microsoft) appeal to the brain. Margins tend to be small in brain-appealing businesses—there is one lowest price or fastest processor. Second, *the heart*: we have an innate desire to connect with the people around us. "Choosy moms choose Jif." Caring for those around you makes you more willing to spend. Third, *the gut*: ever since our caveman days, we have worked to accumulate the most resources for the least output. Our modern lives depend on a steady supply of stuff. Finally, *the genitals*: one of our most primordial instincts, that of propagating our species. We are motivated to buy products and services that make us feel more successful and good-looking, so we can attract better mates. We pay irrational margins for products that improve our sex appeal. Contrast rational companies Walmart and Amazon (the brain and the gut) to Ferrari and Louboutin (the genitals).

**Accelerant.** A firm that serves as an incredible springboard for a person's career. Other than intellectual property or defensible IP, a firm's ability to attract talented employees is one of the most important contributors to success.

**Balancing growth and margins.** Today's most successful firms maintain explosive growth and strong margins. Typically speaking, margins are in conflict with growth. There are some companies that take very low margins, like Walmart, and as a result are able to grow faster because they don't charge much additional margin for their value-add. In contrast, if a firm has high margins, it usually has lower growth and lower potential for scaling. Only some exceptional firms, like the Four, are able to combine high growth with high margins.

**Rundle.** A bundle of goods and/or services that justifies recurring revenue. This strategy exploits one of our key weaknesses as human beings: we are terrible at estimating the value of time. Firms that convince consumers to enter into a monogamous relationship with them are positioned to accumulate more value over time than firms that interact with consumers transactionally. An example of a rundle: Apple currently offers music and streaming video subscriptions, but it could bundle both of those products, plus news, plus annual iPhone upgrades, into a bigger recurring revenue bundle.[5] Disney could bundle Disney+, parks, cruises, and other perks into several tiers of packages based on recurring revenue, or a multiple-product subscription.

**Vertical integration.** A firm's ability to control the end-to-end customer experience by controlling as much of the value chain as possible. Companies that control distribution reap huge benefits. Take Apple. By controlling the App Store and the iPhone, the firm takes a cut of every dime spent on third-party apps. It sells its products through 500 brand temples known as Apple Stores, and over the next two years will shift to designing all its key silicon in-house.

**Benjamin Button products.** Products or services that age in reverse (get more, rather than less, valuable to users over time) due to network effects. Unlike traditional products, like cars or toothpaste, which depreciate in value almost immediately after purchase, Benjamin Button products get more valuable with time and with additional users. For example, on Spotify, more artists means more users, which means more personalization of playlists, including sharing your playlists with friends, which makes it that much more fun for you to be on Spotify, which draws more artists, etc.

**Visionary storytelling.** The ability to articulate or demonstrate progress against a bold vision for the company to shareholders and stakeholders. Telling a compelling story unites employees and attracts top talent and cheap capital. But it's not enough only to inspire—the firm has to actually deliver on its promises.

**Likability.** The ability of a company's leaders to insulate the firm from government and media scrutiny, strike favorable partnerships, and attract top talent. Consumers tend to personify brands, and those that can take on positive, animate characteristics tend to reap outsized benefit.

## THE SHINIEST UNICORNS IN THE HERD

Using the T Algorithm, and considering the disruptability of their industries, here are some companies, both public and private, that I'm following:

**Airbnb.** In 2018, I said Airbnb was the most innovative consumer tech firm of the year, monetizing the largest asset class in the world (U.S. real estate) without owning or maintaining the asset—this enables it to spend more on customer acquisition in social and search, resulting in more web traffic than hotel peers. Unlike Uber, Airbnb is monetizing a fallow asset vs. drivers' need for flexibility and their willingness to accept low wages and no benefits.

The pandemic's immediate impact on Airbnb was a significant decline in revenue, but its asset-light model means the disruptor's costs can be variabilized, since unlike hotel firms, they have no interest on mortgages, upkeep costs, or expensive employee benefits costs. In sum, Airbnb can roll with the punches, while peer hotels just get punched. After a 67% drop in revenue in Q2, Airbnb saw more nights booked for U.S. listings between May 17 and June 3 than the same period in 2019, and a similar boost in domestic travel globally.[6] Airbnb is expected to file to go public before the end of 2020, and we believe it will likely be one of the most valuable firms in travel/hospitality on the offering. The space demands global supply and demand (people from all over the world book places to stay in Austin), and Airbnb has it. This is the definition of a moat.

**Brooklinen.** In 2015, one of my students asked me to invest in his business. He was sourcing cotton in Egypt, milling it in Israel, and then landing a set of sheet sets, duvets, and pillows in Brooklyn for $79 that he would sell for $129. The value proposition was clear: bedding that sold elsewhere at $400, for a lot less. The Fulops, a husband-and-wife team, had secured orders online before the cotton was purchased. This is the definition of good marketing and business strategy—finding products for your consumers vs. finding consumers for your products (piling stuff high in a store and hoping people buy). Streamlining the supply chain to offer better value on a better product is gangster. Today, their company, Brooklinen, is profitable, and sold to Summit Partners in March at a multiple of revenues—rare for retail. Nice sheets, too.

**Carnival.** Not a disruptor, but nonetheless a company to watch post corona. In the months before the pandemic, Carnival was trading around $50 a share, but in August, it was under $14. For good reason—the company's operations are entirely shut down, until at least October 31. But there will be a post-pandemic world, and as long as we keep making old people, cruise lines will be fine. The cruise industry was the fastest-growing segment in the leisure travel market, with demand increasing 62% between 2005 and 2015. And cruisers just want to keep on cruising. Back when it was an option, 92% of cruisers said they would book a cruise as their next vacation. What's powering that is a combination of demographics (more old people) and a classic value proposition: edited selection. Rookie marketers think people want choice. Consumers don't want more choice, but more confidence in the choices presented. Choice is a tax on time and attention. Customers want someone else to do the research and curate the options for them. You could try to merchandise a better itinerary on a boat through Southeast Asia (hotels, meals, activities, planes, trains, cars), or you can let Carnival figure it out for you.

The stock has taken a substantial hit, and there's a chance the pandemic will last longer than Carnival can stay liquid. But the stock triples if the firm survives, making it an interesting cyclical vs. structural trade. The demand destruction in cruises is cyclical, vs. airline travel or restaurant patronage, which is likely structural, as we'll be home more for a long time.

**Lemonade.** A quintessential 2020 disruptor. (Disclosure: I'm an investor.) The firm's sector—insurance—has not changed its offering in decades and has amassed an ocean of consumer ill will. Digitizing the supply chain sheds expensive distribution costs (like insurance salespeople), and the firm is using artificial intelligence to achieve better loss ratios (i.e., better risk assessment). Incumbents don't seem worried, as Lemonade is now just a small renters-insurance operation, barely nipping at the heels of the big players. But even a small improvement in customer experience is an edge, and the capital markets will provide Lemonade the resources to turn that edge into dragon stone.

Lemonade appeals to the brain—you can get insurance quotes in minutes. It meets our desire for answers and for efficiency of information, similar to Google. It also, stay with me here, foots to our instinct to procreate. Herding with "innovators" is similar to hanging with the cool kids at lunch as you hope some of that sheen makes you more attractive to others. And Lemonade has a rundle, a recurring revenue relationship with customers, who pay monthly premiums. Its likability is strong—the CEO has deftly incorporated a social mission that refunds unused reserves for claims to a charity of the customer's choosing. The net/net is higher NPS compared to legacy insurance providers including State Farm, Liberty Mutual, Allstate, etc. In June I said that Lemonade's IPO would be a "monster," and it was the best performing IPO (to date) of 2020, repricing up just before it issued, and still increasing 140% in the first two days of trading.[7]

**Netflix.** Streaming video during a pandemic is a good place to be. The space has attracted incremental investment that rivals the defense budgets of G7 countries. But Netflix has made equally staggering investments over the last decade. The streaming video firms accomplished something only Amazon has managed in recent years: first they achieved a near-zero cost of capital through exceptional storytelling, then they maintained that superpower while shifting from a growth story to a margin story. This is hard. It's relatively easy to get super-low-cost capital when you're growing like a weed. The challenge is when the growth peaks and capital markets begin looking at the bottom of the income statement.

Netflix has used that capital not just to build out its streaming infrastructure (which is impressive enough), but to recast what "value" means in entertainment: For every dollar per month, the consumer receives a billion dollars' worth of content. A $10 movie ticket to a $100-million movie gets you a mere $10 million per dollar, and you can only access it for two hours. Netflix gives you a 100 times the value with on-demand access in a theater that has captured more capital investment and innovation than any chain of multiplexes: your living room.

It's unlikely you will watch 1% of what's available (note: I'm trying), but the most prevalent application of AI (the Netflix recommendation engine) brings a Facebook/Google-like cocktail of scale and targeting that makes the Los Gatos firm the Herschel Walker of tech—enormous, yet fast. Netflix innovates around the notion of scale better than any content company. At its production facility in Madrid, the firm has assembled a content machine 10,000 people strong. Yet the model is such that Netflix Madrid will produce the content of an even larger operation. Same story, screenwriting, cinematography, set, and costume design, but several scenes shot with the "it" actors from various regions produces more relevant content, faster. Again, Herschel Walker. Netflix has busted free from the narcissistic U.S. belief that the world wants to keep seeing American actors. No, they want American scale and cheap capital with regionalized talent.

In 2011, I bought a lot of shares (for a professor) of Netflix at $12 a share. That's the good news. The bad: I sold at $10 a share to take the tax loss and never repurchased. The shares hover around $500 as I write. I want to clone myself, find a time machine, go back in time, and slap myself in the face. But I digress.

Okay, what about a firm you likely haven't heard of?

**One Medical.** I think One Medical is a disruptor and has many of the features that signal potential for extraordinary returns.

Some of the weapons of mass entrenchment in healthcare (like HIPAA compliance) have been somewhat eroded due to the urgent need to streamline healthcare delivery. Just as retail added hundreds of billions in value via the adoption of multichannel, healthcare's embrace of smartphones, cameras, and speakers will unlock staggering value.

Imagine you're camping and your kid steps on a wasp and his foot starts to swell. You immediately want to pull someone up on your phone and then have them give you the confidence to say, "Okay, you need to pack up the tents and get here." Or say, "No. You're fine. Wash the area with soap, and then soak his foot in that cold mountain lake behind you. Tomorrow drive into town and get this antihistamine, the prescription has been electronically sent to a pharmacy geolocated to your phone." Less cost, more time with family, and peace of mind.

The aspects of healthcare that stands to recognize the greatest benefits of Covid-inspired innovation are those where change has been resisted through inertia. Innovative service delivery is one such area. One Medical offers healthcare through the channels the industry has resisted—specifically, the handheld phone. The technology removes friction, costs, stigma, and increases privacy.

**Peloton.** This rally will outlive the coronavirus. The $1 billion revenue firm defines the T Algorithm: I initially felt the firm was overvalued, and then . . . Covid hit.

YOY growth of 69%. Recurring revenue is at the heart of its

business model, and there's nothing like a $2,000 bike to make a $39 monthly fee seem reasonable. Benjamin Button (network) effects are at work—the more customers, the greater the benefits from the (rabid) community.

Peloton is approaching 1 million connected subscribers, with a Netflix/Prime-like 93% retention rate,[8] better margins than Apple, and vertical control over its offering. Because it can leverage its instructors across so many more customers, Peloton is a career accelerant for its instructors, whom it poaches from the likes of SoulCycle and Equinox, offering triple the compensation, equity, and a platform that offers exposure to thousands online.

**Investing Apps: Public and Robinhood.** Financial services is an industry ripe for disruption, and the pandemic has boosted personal stock trading activity as many people have more time on their hands, and an additional $1,200 in their bank accounts. Robinhood is the big name here, and when it introduced commission-free trading, established players were forced to respond and abolish commissions. This likely prompted the merger of industry leaders Charles Schwab and TD Ameritrade. Robinhood also added fractional share trading, letting its mostly young user base buy into expensive stocks they might not otherwise own. More than half of the app's users are first-time investors, and the interface is gamified in a way that encourages more time on the app. Splashy visuals, random rewards (badges, high-yield checking accounts unlocked if you tap on this icon

100 times, etc.), the dopa hits of a video game—or casino. The company embodies big tech's evolution from innovation (better products) to exploitation (depressed teens, gamification, addicting young people to variable rewards). Why not, it works for Facebook. Gamification is an exploitation algorithm, as is the enragement algorithm that controls the Facebook newsfeed.

Public is taking a different approach to commission free, user-friendly, fractional-share trading apps. (Disclosure: I'm an investor.) But Public views itself as a social network that provides stock trading, and emphasizes communication among users in public forums and private chats. At sufficient scale, a network of connected users becomes an asset, and one that—at a certain scale—competitors will struggle to match.

How about a firm that is all show and no go?

**Quibi.** The most compelling content from Quibi is . . . Quibi. This debacle is worth watching, as it illuminates several insights about our ecosystem. First, tech entrepreneurship is a young person's game (ageist . . . and true). One of Quibi's advertised strengths was the leadership of Meg Whitman and Jeffrey Katzenberg. And why not? They are first-ballot Hall of Famers in tech and storytelling, respectively. However, to my knowledge, there's never been a successful media-tech firm founded by people in their sixties. The young brain is crazy, creative, and willing to work 80 hours a week—young people think they'll live forever. People in their sixties are not blessed or cursed with any of these things, which makes them decent leaders, great mentors, and lousy entrepreneurs. Second, you can't compete against the Four without either a 10 times better product or access to capital that dwarfs the incumbents. I'm sure $1 billion (increased to $1.75 billion) felt like a lot to Hollywood veteran Katzenberg when he signed on. However, at Amazon, $1.75 billion is "a pretty good day," and it's what Netflix spends on original content in 5 weeks.[9]

**Shopify.** Shopify is the most impressive tech company of the last decade, and perhaps the most courageous. The Canadian firm recognized the huge white space to become the anti-Amazon Amazon. Similar to Amazon's Pay and FBA (Fulfillment by Amazon) products, Shopify provides payment and fulfillment for third-party retailers. Unlike Amazon, however, Shopify's CEO could honestly tell Congress it doesn't use the data it collects from third-party retailers to inform its own competitive product sales. Shopify disrupts Amazon by offering customers the service and value of Amazon without the data and branding exploitation. The result? A $131 billion market cap, up 6 times since the beginning of 2019. Shopify has outperformed Amazon stock YTD (+250% vs. +72%).

**Spotify.** Spotify boasts global reach, product differentiation, and likability. It lacks vertical integration and is perpetually punished for that by Apple, which skims 30% in App Store commission. In 2018, I predicted the stock would double in

12 months. I was wrong, it took 30. But Spotify still has all the makings of a potential trillion-dollar firm. They have recurring revenue and a Benjamin Button product—it ages in reverse and appreciates, rather than depreciates, with time and increased use.

But even with these assets, Spotify's stock hasn't reached big tech status with a market cap of $47 billion. What's holding the Swedish firm back? Apple Music. The Cupertino giant has half the paid subscribers and inferior NPS scores. But most of the music available on Spotify is also available on Apple Music, and Apple Music has a key advantage—it's vertical, controlling its own distribution.

The gangster move? Netflix and Spotify merge and acquire Sonos for vertical integration. The two mob families of subscription media consolidate to control video and music. Gangster. They acquire Sonos (with the sweat of their *Tiger*[10] brow at $1.3 billion) and establish a vertical beachhead of devices in the wealthiest homes in America.

**Tesla.** Appealing to human instinct: Tesla has several points of differentiation—Elon Musk's vision and storytelling, combined with a tangibly better product, have provided the firm with capital at a cost that renders other automobile manufacturers flaccid, as they can't make the same forward-leaning investments as the Alameda firm. While Ford is running commercials on NFL reruns on TNT, Elon has NASA astronauts drive a Tesla Model X to the launch pad, where they will board a

SpaceX Dragon spaceship. The firm is also vertical, selling cars directly. Does anybody really miss going to an auto dealership? But Tesla's true kryptonite is its best-in-class ability to command irrational margins by appealing to a core human instinct— procreation. Buying a Tesla is the ultimate status symbol. Most products indicate one of two things: "I'm rich" or "I have a conscience." But Tesla does what only philanthropy offers . . . both. Plus, it says: I'm an innovator. I'm ahead of the curve. Put another way, I have genes paramount to the survival of the species; you have a biological imperative to mate with me. And the bad-boy image adds to the procreation-instinct appeal of the car. That tax lawyer driving a Model S isn't a tax lawyer, he's a visionary rebel.

Tesla appeals to the genitals through every aspect of its strategy: pricing, production, marketing, and even its leadership. Elon Musk is a genius. I don't respect many of his personal choices: market manipulation ("funding secured"), calling the Thai cave diver "a pedo," then insisting he was right, and tweets questioning Covid measures. The founder of a firm on which thousands of livelihoods depend should be more measured and mindful—I know, "ok boomer."

I've said for years (and been wrong) that Tesla is overvalued. Now I prefer to say that it is "fully valued." Keeps the hate mail down. Yes, Musk is a genius. Yes, Tesla has changed the world for the better through alternative energy. However, at the end of the day, it's bending steel, and that's not a business that can support a (double checking my notes) 128 times multiple of EBITDA.

Aswath Damodaran, my colleague at the NYU Stern School of Business, who is dubbed the "Dean of Valuation," says, "I've always thought of Tesla as a story stock. It's the story that drives the price, not the news, and not the fundamentals. . . . If you're trading Tesla based on expected earnings or cash flow, you're trading it for the wrong reasons. People trade Tesla based on mood and momentum." Tesla is benefiting from the fact that Covid-19 has had a disproportionately negative effect on older, capital-intensive companies. In a sense, the virus has handicapped Tesla's competition. That explains why the young electric-car companies are doing better than the established automobile companies, which have lots of debt and huge capital intensity. That's exactly it—Tesla is in the auto sector, and in that sector, valuations like these don't make sense. "People who buy Tesla aren't irrational, it's just not a rationality I buy into," Professor Damodaran said. "Tesla is an implausible story but not an impossible story. There is a story you can tell that will justify a $1,500 stock price, but it's not a story I want to bet on."[11]

**Twitter.** (Disclosure: I am a shareholder.) If Twitter commanded the space it occupies, it would be a $100-billion-dollar company (vs. $30 billion). The microblogging platform has become an iconic brand and the global heartbeat for our information age. The only firms with the reach and influence of Twitter

(Tencent, Facebook, and Google) register 17, 24, and 39 times the market capitalization, respectively. This is an embarrassment, and management is to blame. Half to blame, since CEO Jack Dorsey is only part time. Or does that make him doubly to blame?

Twitter has a lot of negatives: fake accounts, GRU-sponsored trolls, algorithms that promote conspiracies and junk science, and inconsistent application of the terms of service, to name a few. Users regularly refer to it as a *hellsite* and being on it as *doomscrolling*. But none of these are why it can't turn on the profit engines. All this and worse hasn't stopped Facebook. The problem is the model. Twitter is stubbornly clinging to an advertising business, but it doesn't have the scale or the tools to compete with Facebook and Google. As a result it has all the problems of being in the free/red/Android camp, without the scale advantages.

In December 2019, I purchased 330,000 shares and wrote an open letter to Twitter's board of directors, which can be found at profgalloway.com/twtr-enough-already.

Shocker: I didn't get a response. However, a couple of months later Elliott Management (a hedge fund with $38 billion under management) informed me they had essentially signed my letter with a $2-billion pen, and 3 weeks later they were granted 3 seats on the board. In the world of activist investing, securing 3 seats in 3 weeks means the company knows it doesn't have a leg to stand on (see above: part-time CEO). I am advising Elliott, and my advice has been well publicized.

Twitter needs to go iOS—charge for value vs. exploit for data. It needs to move to a subscription model, as I described in chapter 1. Free for accounts under 2,000 followers, then a sliding scale that starts small, but as the value to the user of having a big audience starts to kick in, the subscription fees rise accordingly.

I had been calling for Twitter to do this for months when Jack announced a move toward subscription in July 2020. The stock popped 4%. A full-time CEO would have figured it out sooner.

**Uber.** Ride hailing is the tobacco of the gig economy and the most recent battle waged by the lords against the serfs in the U.S. We've sequestered the mostly non-white, mostly non-college-educated drivers (3.9 million of them) from the mostly white, mostly college-educated employees (22,000 of them) at HQ, who will split, with their investors, the value of BMW and Ford. By the way, BMW and Ford employ 334,000 people. Pretty sure most have health insurance. The average hourly wage at Ford is $26 an hour. At Uber, it's $9 an hour.

Unlike Lyft, which will either be acquired or go out of business, Uber has a global brand and has demonstrated a flywheel—Uber Eats. With the purchase of Postmates in July 2020, amid the pandemic, the flywheel gets stronger. If Uber leverages their formidable brand, culture of innovation, and flywheel, it could be worth $40 billion, even $50 billion—a 50% decline from its pricing on the eve of the IPO. In its favor during Covid is its ability to variabilize costs. Uber's capacity to extend beyond ride hailing is key, because ride hailing is a difficult business. But even a bad business can be a flywheel if you get big enough and develop a sufficiently lucrative business model. Contrast with Lyft, which is actually trying to make a business out of ride hailing, sub-scale. Acquired, most likely in 2021.

Uber has a Benjamin Button effect—the more people that use the algo, the better it gets. The more drivers, the lower the rates, and the more accurate the maps, time estimates, and other aspects of the algorithm. In terms of likability, Uber has had quite a bit to repair after the founding CEO, Travis Kalanick, wrecked the brand's image with a bro culture made famous by a young female engineer, Susan Fowler. Leather jackets for all employees . . . except women.[12] Dara Khosrowshahi has been a vast improvement and has dealt with a row of crises in a resolute manner. In terms of vertical integration, Uber's strength (minimal CapEx) is also its soft tissue, as it doesn't own cars or have exclusive driver contracts. Many, if not most, Uber drivers also drive for Lyft. Uber's growth has been strong. Even if it's not currently profitable, margins are improving.

**Warby Parker.** The incumbent (EssilorLuxottica) has raised prices and not innovated—offering hundreds of millions, maybe billions, in unearned margin up for grabs. Despite a sector, specialty retail, that's been hammered, Warby will be a rare retail IPO of 2021.

Warby is the least bad start-up in specialty retail, a sector that has been a wonderful place to shop and a terrible place to invest or work. The firm tells a great story that garners huge PR, as evidenced by Casper and Away needing to pay to generate traffic while Warby Parker gets nearly 80% of its traffic organically. Warby looks to have the muscle (vertical distribution, differentiated product) and fat (access to cheap capital) to survive an Amazon winter and emerge stronger.

**WeWork.** No, really. The concept works (coworking) but needs to be right-sized. Restructuring may be in store for many unicorns who have a decent business at their core, but just got way over their skis. They need to think like the real estate business they are. For example, hotels are usually separate LLCs so one hotel can declare bankruptcy without taking down the whole company. Smart. If WeWork can shed its bad assets (step one, fire the founder, done) coworking has a bright post-pandemic future. Many of America's office workers have been freed of the office, but not everyone wants to work at their kitchen table. Expect to see "Remote with Cowork Stipend" appearing on the comp line of more and more job descriptions, and companies limiting their permanent footprints drastically, relying instead on flexible space arrangements with partners like We-Work 2.0. *We* was never worth $47 billion, but it may be worth more than its Covid valuation.

**TikTok.** I'm less certain about what will happen with Tik Tok than what will not happen. Despite a lot of sound and fury in the summer of 2020, the Chinese will not be bullied by the Trump administration into selling a global internet asset on the cheap. For one thing, China has ample means to counterattack against Trump's threat to ban TikTok. Imagine if President Xi Jinping announced, "The iPhone circumvents Chinese security protocols. Apple must sell its operations in China, intellectual property rights, and supply chain agreements to a Chinese firm within 45 days." Goodbye, NASDAQ recovery. Not to mention people *like* TikTok. Including quite a few people who vote. And indeed, even as this book goes to press, Trump has already extended his 45-day deadline for TikTok's U.S. assets to be sold to an American company to a 90-day deadline. The Chinese government has positioned itself to call Trump's bluff by requiring TikTok to get its approval before selling to a foreign company, and Microsoft, the likeliest and most logical suitor, has dropped out of the bidding. This chapter of the saga will likely be over by the time you read this, but right now, the best Trump can hope for is a face-saving "partnership" between Oracle and ByteDance with vague terms designed to placate Beijing, not Washington.

In the meantime, the furor has been a great chance for companies to juice their stock prices by letting rumors circulate about their own supposed interest in the company. Twitter's stock jumped 5%, only to slide back once investors did the math and realized any deal would mean that ByteDance would effectively be buying Twitter, in light of Twitter's relatively small valuation. You have to love the unintended consequences there—trying to acquire TikTok for an American company, Trump could have ended up facilitating Twitter's sale to a Chinese one.

The bottom line is that TikTok has a great product. The algorithm is brilliant at surfacing new, relevant content, and the content creation tools ensure there is plenty such content queued up. This is not easy—look at Reels, Facebook's (predictable) rip-off feature recently added to Instagram. *New York Times* internet culture writer Taylor Lorenz tried it for five days and concluded: "I can definitively say Reels is the worst feature I've ever used."[13] Great products find their way into great businesses, and whether as a Microsoft product (and Redmond, to its credit, has managed not to ruin Minecraft, Skype, or LinkedIn, all high-profile acquisitions that continue to thrive) or on its own, TikTok has a bright potential future. Similar to the poorly executed trade war, China will not blink first, as they blink less often—they think in 50-year time horizons.

VENTURE CAPITAL INVESTMENTS have largely recovered to pre-Covid levels.[14] We've been in a slow-moving technology revolution for most of my adult life, but only recently has the infrastructure and technology advanced to the point where the widespread disruption we've been expecting for decades started to shake the roots of the largest consumer sectors in the economy. As opportunities arise, the private markets are flush with capital, the public markets are hungry for growth stories, and the potential acquirers have deeper pockets than ever (though antitrust may dampen the ardor of big tech acquisitions for a while). Again, I believe the 2020–21 IPO class will be one of the best-performing vintages of the last several years. The successes will wallpaper over an uncomfortable truth: some of the fastest-growing sectors in our economy have scant start-up funding, as the incumbents have not been subject to the same antitrust or regulatory scrutiny as firms in the past.

You've likely noticed that a key to a firm's success is the inertia of the incumbents. There are few industries as big and immobile as higher education in the U.S.

# HIGHER EDUCATION

Few industries sit closer to the ground zero of Covid acceleration than higher education. Even before the pandemic, the $700 billion business (and, to be clear, this is a business) was ripe for disruption. For decades, higher education has been sticking its chin farther and farther out. Covid-19 will be the fist that meets it. The virus has been especially hard on industries whose customers consume the product sitting shoulder to shoulder, like sports, airlines, restaurants, events—and despite their noble mission, universities.

## Ripe for Disruption

The disruptability index for higher education is off the charts. In the past 40 years, college tuition has increased 1,400%. In the 1980s and early '90s, I attended five years of undergrad at UCLA and two years of business school at UC Berkeley for a grand total of $10,000 in tuition—all seven years. Fast forward to present day, that won't cover two classes at NYU Stern ($14,000).

## COLLEGE TUITION & FEES VS. CPI
### JULY 1978–JULY 2020

COLLEGE TUITION & FEES     CONSUMER PRICE INDEX

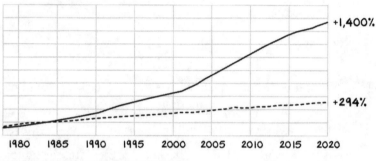

+1,400%

+294%

1980   1985   1990   1995   2000   2005   2010   2015   2020

SOURCE: US BUREAU OF LABOR STATISTICS.

Compared to this, even healthcare seems like a bargain. Healthcare spending has "only" increased 600% in the same period.[1] What has the education industry done with this extraordinary transfer of wealth? Not much. We rightly complain about healthcare costs increasing, but if you go to a hospital today, the technology, procedures, and medications are substantially different than in 1980. Our nearly $4-trillion-a-year healthcare industry provides cutting-edge training and technology. Have outcomes kept pace with price increases? No. But there has been substantial innovation.

Our $600-billion higher education industry, in contrast, offers a product so old it's comforting. Venture into a university class today. The fashion is different, there's PowerPoint vs. transparencies, and the kids have laptops and Diet Cokes vs. legal pads and Tab. But that's about it.

I teach brand strategy at NYU's Stern School of Business. This fall, on Zoom, the class is almost twice the usual size at 280 kids (what I affectionately call students). They are paying $7,000 each. That's $1.96 million for the semester. Conservatively, the gross margins on this course are 90+ points. Name another business, at this price point, that registers 90% gross margins. Few if any have been able to achieve these economics. Not Hermès, not Ferrari, not Apple.

I'm decent at what I do, sometimes even good. Once or twice a semester I deliver a session online—so I can travel, but also to explore the online medium. I do what I can to keep students engaged, from impersonating rock stars to sending intemperate emails to rude students.[2] But underneath the Adele wig,[3] my class is not much different from the brand strategy class I took from David Aaker at Berkeley Haas 28 years ago. I stand at the front of the room, I dispense my wisdom for three hours, and NYU collects a check. Not in that order.

## SCARCITY

How has my industry raised prices at this rate without improving the product? At a few elite institutions, including NYU, we've leveraged scarcity. More than a business strategy, it's become a fetish—believing you are a luxury brand instead of a public servant. Ivy Leagues have acceptance rates of 4–10%. A university president bragging about rejecting 90% of applicants is tantamount to a homeless shelter taking pride in turning away 90% of the needy that arrive each night. And this is not about standards or brand dilution. In an essay explaining his decision to stop conducting application interviews for his alma mater, Princeton, journalist Bryan Walsh observed, "The secret of elite college admissions is that far more students deserve to attend these colleges than are admitted, and there is virtually no discernible difference between those who make it and the many more who just miss out." In support, he offered this statement from Princeton's own dean of admissions: "We could have admitted five or six classes to Princeton from the [applicant] pool."[4]

So, with a $26 billion endowment, the question becomes, Why wouldn't you?

The excess demand feeds into the cartel of higher ed. Hundreds of private, liberal arts colleges that offer a facsimile of the Harvard aesthetic have drafted off the price increases of the elites (and the 95% of families rejected), giving millions of middle-class families the opportunity to purchase a Hyundai for the price of a Mercedes. Much of this is financed with easy-to-obtain credit, exploiting a uniquely held American belief that has morphed into scripture: You've sinned as a parent unless you get your kid through college . . . at any cost.

Meanwhile, at the hundreds of public institutions around

the country that educate two thirds of our college graduates, tuition increases have been fueled by a reduction in state and federal funding. Though it varies from state to state, on average, public funding per student is lower today than it was in 1980. The 2008 recession in particular triggered deep cuts: between 2008 and 2013, public funding had been cut by 22%—and tuition was up 27%. Some of this is our own fault. Colleges have embraced people who do not look like us, but are increasingly intolerant of people who don't think like us. Only 1.5% of Harvard faculty identify as conservative.[5] The result is that about 50% of elected officials are disinclined to fund a progressive orthodoxy.

The pain of budget cuts is not evenly distributed. Alabama, for example, slashed funding for its university system by nearly 40% during the recession and has never restored that funding.[6] The system has had to make up the difference in tuition increases, and by heavily recruiting out-of-state and international students—profoundly altering the nature of the institution and its role in the community it is supposed to serve.

## ABUNDANCE

All these price increases have been enabled by the heroin of federally subsidized student loans. Student loan debt now totals $1.6 trillion, far more than credit-card debt or auto loans. The average graduate will carry nearly $30,000 in debt away from their virtual graduation.

## TOTAL DEBT HELD BY AMERICANS
Q2 2020

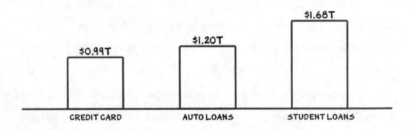

SOURCE: FEDERAL RESERVE BANK OF ST. LOUIS.

The cheap credit has enriched some institutions, permitted states to cut support for others, and loaded rising generations with grotesque amounts of debt. It's a program that belongs in the Hall of Fame for good intentions and bad outcomes: debt-fueled increases in tuition and the rise of predatory for-profit colleges, with little appreciable increase in the quality of the product. Crucially, it has failed in its core mission—the expansion of college education to people of lesser means. In fact, the burden of debt has fallen most harshly on the lower economic strata, who default at far higher rates than wealthier students.[7]

## IVY-COVERED CASTE SYSTEM

We like to position education as the great leveler. But in fact it has become a caste system, a means of passing privilege on to the next generation. Sure, we let in a few freakishly remarkable kids from the masses so we can pretend to be a meritocracy, but between legacy admissions, high school inequality, and straight up pay-to-play arrangements, the wealthy are wildly overrepresented in our colleges. Wealthy kids today are over twice as likely to go to college as poor kids, and over *five times as likely* to attend an elite school.[8] At 38 of the top 100 colleges in America, including 5 of the Ivies, there are more students from the top 1% of income than there are from the bottom 60%.[9] You could argue that at this point, the Ivy League undergraduate programs are not colleges, but hedge funds that educate the children of their investors.

Even for those privileged few, college is still a great investment. Top college graduates are launched into an entirely different career and income trajectory than the rest of America. The most sought-after employers recruit them; their career counseling departments get their phone calls returned, and once in jobs, college friends and alumni networks stock senior management.

## DISRUPTIVE FORCES

Just below the surface of the most disruptable industry, several trends have been accelerating. Technological improvements have brought distance learning to the threshold of market acceptance. An early 2000s burst of interest in MOOCs (massive, open, online courses) proved premature, but there are plenty of other sharks bumping the prey. The best brands in the industry— Harvard, Yale, Stanford, MIT—have been steadily expanding their online offerings. At Harvard, David Malan has made the school's renowned introductory computer science course into an international phenomenon, taking it online and tuition-free. In 2018, 1,200 students enrolled in Yale professor Lauri Santos's course "Psychology and the Good Life," making it the most popular in the school's 300-year history. But when Santos and Yale put the course online, for free, over *one million* people enrolled.[10] Coming from another direction, MasterClass has brought the power of celebrity and Hollywood production to online education. I don't think their model works—Anna Wintour vomiting platitudes is not education—but the production values have inspired an increase in quality across online learning.

Meanwhile, the student debt crisis has spurred a widespread rethinking of the traditional college value proposition. Bernie Sanders and Elizabeth Warren put free college at the center of their platforms. As bad an idea as this would be—another transfer of wealth from the poor to the rich, as college attendees skew wealthy—it's a recognition that we need to make college more affordable.

Demographics are destiny, and higher education's demographic picture is ugly. Beginning in 2026, the number of graduating high school seniors is projected to decline by 9%.[11] Change is coming. In 2013, renowned Harvard Business School professor Clayton Christensen predicted that online education would disrupt traditional higher education just as steam power had put sailing ships out of business. Over the next ten to fifteen years, he wrote, 25% of colleges and universities would go out of business.[12] By 2018, he'd upped his prediction to 50%.[13] And that was before anyone had heard of Covid-19.

Higher education has resisted change. Its hold on our imagination is strong—the vision of young people strolling in leafy quads, minds on fire from challenging academic inspiration. Its brand strength is extraordinary. No one gives $100 million to put their name on the side of a building on Google's campus. Nearly every politician, donor, and thought leader holds fond memories of years spent at one or more of these institutions, and plans for their offspring to enjoy the same benefits. And for all the promise of technology and the risks of elitism, the traditional model of higher education is not easily replicated.

And then the pandemic hit. Almost overnight, American colleges emptied out, and millions of hours of classroom experience shifted abruptly online. Lecture halls were left for childhood bedrooms, leafy quads deserted for suburban backyards and socially distanced walks. Hardly anyone was ready for this, and our first pass at online learning was a buggy, Zoom-bombed, dreary mess. A nation of parents saw their $40,000-per-year education put its worst foot forward and were underwhelmed. Students lost one of "the best years of their lives." After a spring semester of upheaval and ad hoc Zoom classes, 75% of college students were unhappy with e-learning,[14] and 1 in 6 high school seniors were considering deferring college for a semester or a year.[15]

# The Crisis Is Upon Us

For much of the spring and early summer 2020, we heard a lot of happy talk from university leadership claiming campus life would return to near-normal in the fall. It was never going to happen. In late July, the dominos started to fall, as school after school announced that they would begin the 2020–21 academic year online—for most schools, a reversal of their springtime optimism. From large state universities including UC Berkeley, to small private colleges like Smith College, to research institutions like Johns Hopkins, and the wealthiest elite schools like Harvard, Princeton, and Stanford, schools of all stripes accepted the inevitable and announced they would hold no in-person courses in late August and offer severely limited on-campus housing. As this book goes to press in late September, the College Crisis Initiative reports that 1,302 of the 2,958 schools that it tracks plan on a fully or primarily online Fall 2020 (up from 835 just a month earlier).[16] Only 114 schools plan a fully on-campus program. We are in for at least a year of radically transformed higher education, and much of the change will be permanent.

Understanding the pandemic effect on higher education requires understanding higher education's value proposition. In exchange for time and tuition, college offers three components of value: a *credential*, an *education*, and an *experience*.

# (C + E + EX) / TUITION

**C** = Credential (the lane you are put in post-graduation based on the brand/school you attended)

**E** = Education (learning and stuff)

**Ex** = Experience (fall leaves, football games, falling in love)

## FISCAL SHOCK

The pandemic will accelerate change in higher education in two waves. In the first, which hit the industry in late summer 2020, many institutions experienced fiscal shock. Even Harvard, with its 4.6% admission rate and its $40 billion endowment, is projecting a $750 million revenue shortfall for fiscal year 2020 and is asking employees to consider early retirement or reduced schedules.[17] That said, elite institutions have substantial shock absorbers: waitlist and multibillion-dollar endowments. For every student who takes a gap year or transfers to be closer to home, there are ten more who want the seat. The elite universities will weather the storm and emerge stronger.

But when the top schools fill their pandemic revenue hole by going deep into their waitlist, that will exacerbate the problem for less prestigious schools, who incur a double whammy of decreasing yield (percentage of student admittees who enroll) as some applicants get off the waiting list of a more prestigious school while others decide to defer. The effect will ripple down the rankings, until it hits schools that don't have a waitlist. Schools that already admit 60 or 80% of their applicants have no reserve, and they are going to go into Fall 2020 and future semesters with a fatal number of empty seats. Moreover, schools with low yields face an additional challenge. Their admissions decisions are reliant on complex predictive models regarding which students will actually attend, and it is critical they accurately calibrate how many of those students will require financial aid. As Kevin Carey of New America put it, "The financial solvency of many private colleges now rests on a latticework of probability."[18] A sea change in the nature of their student body renders these models useless and puts schools at risk of trying to provide services to an incoming class that can't afford to pay for them.

In short, schools that offer an exceptional credential will be fine. Schools that offer a solid education at a great price are also well positioned. The Cal State system, which many would argue is the real jewel of California, announced they will be online only. This frees them to focus on the tech and formats to deliver a better online experience. Cal State, which will graduate eight times more students than the entire Ivy League this year, accelerates through Covid, as the experience was never a big part of the equation. Most students commute to school, and the denominator is much lower ($6,000 in-state tuition). So, their value ratio, in a time of corona, leapfrogs expensive liberal arts, campus-based universities.

The schools facing an existential threat are colleges that rely largely on the experience aspect of the value proposition. Similar to movie theaters and cruise ships, which take your money to put you in small, enclosed spaces with strangers, colleges that have invested in nice ships/buildings and depend on kids rejected from better brands are in trouble. Schools that offer an elite-like experience, with elite pricing, but without the credential, are about to experience a reckoning.

## DELUSIONAL

The first half of 2020 saw schools trying to fend off the inevitable by insisting they would continue with on-campus education. They redesigned classrooms, housing, and dining halls to permit social distancing, reconfigured their schedules, and established on-campus protocols—no doubt at great cost and effort. Purdue, for example, has reported buying more than a mile of plexiglass to set up barriers all over campus. Outside observers watched all this, incredulous at the notion of keeping thousands of twenty-year-olds socially distanced from one another (if that were possible, the species would have petered out long ago). A psychology professor writing in *The New York Times* called the reopening plans "so unrealistically optimistic that they border on delusional."[19]

Defenders of the return to campus claim that the virus poses little threat to young people. Even if this were true (and it's not), asymptomatic transmission is one of this virus's weapons, and young people—active, mobile, vocal—make for outstanding super-spreaders. Bringing them back to campus puts college towns at risk. Many are not prepared for a surge of infections. Some have permanent populations with high numbers of retirees attracted by the cultural benefits of a nearby college.[20] Other at-risk cohorts include cafeteria workers, maintenance crews, security guards, librarians, bartenders, cabdrivers, their spouses and family members, and anyone else unfortunate enough to have made the once reasonable decision to live in a college town. And if (when) there is an outbreak, the health-care infrastructure of these university towns could be overrun in a matter of weeks, if not days.

## ICU CAPACITY PER 10,000 PEOPLE IN U.S. COLLEGE TOWNS

| | |
|---|---|
| US AVERAGE | 3.6 |
| URBANA, IL | 2.7 |
| LYNCHBURG, VA | 2.5 |
| BLOOMINGTON, IN | 2.1 |
| BINGHAMTON, NY | 1.8 |
| FORT COLLINS, CO | 1.0 |

SOURCE: WASHINGTON POST.

## DESPERATE

Why would college presidents put their students, employees, and neighbors at risk like this? The ugly truth is that many believe they have no choice. College is an expensive operation with a relatively inflexible cost structure. Tenure and union contracts render the largest cost (faculty and administrator salaries) near-immovable objects. The bulk of the teaching is done by adjuncts and assistants, who receive anemic compensation (and grad students, who work for nearly nothing), while the aristocracy of higher ed, the full professors, have their high salaries protected by tenure. In addition, universities have let their non-teaching staff costs bloat obscenely—growing head count is always easier than shrinking it. After working in higher ed for two decades, I believe nearly every decision is made with one goal in mind: how to increase the compensation and decrease the accountability of tenured faculty and administrators.

Government support for education has also been on the decline for generations. The result is that while some universities enjoy revenue streams from technology transfer, hospitals, returns on multibillion-dollar endowments, and public funding, the bulk of colleges have become tuition dependent. If students don't return in any given semester, many colleges will have to take drastic action that could have serious long-term impacts on their ability to fulfill their missions.

So rather than spend the summer of 2020 focused on dramatically improving the online education experience (an investment that would provide returns for decades), university leadership and faculty have spent millions of hours and dollars pursuing a consensual hallucination that they could properly protect their campuses. As Covid infections escalated through the summer—and once schools cashed tuition checks—reality set in, and schools began sobering up.

It may never have been up to them. Many students already decided that the necessary changes to campus life rendered the on-campus experience not worth pursuing and not worth the premium some schools charge for it. In August 2020, one third of college students said they were not planning on going back to campus, and Harvard reported that 20% of its freshmen had asked to defer.

The most consequential absences will be international students—the cash cows of high-tuition universities. We claim we let them in for diversity. True, but that's not the primary motivation for a steady increase in kids from abroad. Two thirds of international students finance their education with money sourced abroad. In aggregate, international students contribute nearly $40 billion annually to the U.S. economy.[21]

## INTERNATIONAL STUDENTS AT US COLLEGES

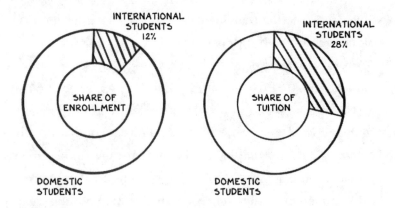

SOURCE: BUSINESS INSIDER.

At NYU, they constitute 27% of our student body and an outsized portion of our cash flow. A pandemic coupled with a Trump administration committed to the demonization of foreigners, including severely limiting the work prospects of highly skilled grad students, may dramatically impact the number of international students applying in future years. This means the whales may just not show up this fall, leaving us with otters and penguins—an enormous fiscal hole.

## DOOMED

The result? We will see a culling among universities. Just as retail closures are accelerating from 9,500 stores in 2019[22] to 25,000+ in 2020,[23] we're going to see hundreds of universities begin a death march. In academia, we have been preying on the hopes and dreams of the middle class, offering parents the chance to check an instinctive box—giving their kids a better life by sending them to college. We also encouraged them to borrow against their 401(k)s and take out mortgages to underwrite our shape-shifting from public servants to luxury brands. No more.

That's the short-term effect. How serious it will be depends on how long it takes to develop and distribute a vaccine. A semester of online education and reduced attendance will kill hundreds of schools. A year without the in-person experience, and the pricing power it brings, could drive 10–30% of universities out of existence.

## The Road Ahead

The long-term effect will be a profound change in the way higher education is delivered in this country. If handled well, it will include a radical opening of the pathways to career success that are currently limited. If handled poorly, it could lead to the transfer of more wealth from the young and working class into the coffers of big tech, and the continued reduction of economic mobility.

The heart of the coming transformation of higher education is technology. As in so many other areas, the pandemic has forced the industry to adopt distance tech that faculty and administrators have resisted. The experience we gain during this period will accelerate adoption.

To be sure, the early phases have not been pretty. Simply taking a college lecture course and putting it on Zoom is not e-learning in any but the most rudimentary sense, and students are predictably dissatisfied. That will change. Schools are putting their faculty through training programs, teaching them how to use the available tools, how to restructure their classes, how to migrate online.

There are some simple things that I've learned are essential. Without the power of physical presence, you have to be much more animated, waving your arms and raising your voice, changing your tone and pace. You have to be in the students' faces, requiring they keep their cameras on. Constantly call on them and seize the opportunity to get better guest speakers, as it's a much easier lift (Zoom vs. commute). Breaking up the monotony of a talking head is essential—learn how to use the screen-sharing function and prepare charts and illustrations that express information in new ways and keep students engaged. A good role model is Rep. Katie Porter's use of small white boards in her congressional hearings.

Online programs offer opportunities beyond the lecture itself. Asynchronous communications using message boards and group documents provide students (and instructors) schedule flexibility that in-person teaching lacks. In-person discussions are a minefield of inequality (research routinely shows that men dominate classroom discussions and that instructors are complicit in the problem). Moving the discussion online is not a panacea (high-speed internet, a laptop, and a quiet place to work are not givens), but it does open up the possibility of engaging students in ways that may be more effective than traditional classroom discussion. New technology that realizes the potential of online instruction while mitigating its downsides is a major opportunity for entrepreneurs. Early in the pandemic, seemingly everyone in America learned about Zoom in the same few days. Going forward, look for companies like Blackboard and Canvas to massively innovate or be replaced. There will be an explosion in new tools and technology hitting the market in the first quarter of 2021 as the tsunami of venture capital being deployed into higher ed takes root.

The crisis has led to an adoption of tech among my colleagues in the last 12 weeks that dwarfs the last 20 years. As former NYU associate dean Anastasia Crosswhite put it, "The median faculty member went from 'online education over my dead body,' to 'I'm not stepping foot in a classroom until there's a vaccine,' within two weeks." And when we finally make it online, we will find our students waiting for us, wondering what took so long. The rising generation has grown up on screens, and is comfortable with online interactions to a degree my generation cannot comprehend.

## SCALE

Schools and professors that take this new medium seriously will garner huge advantage over the next few years, and their stakeholders will benefit. This is not only because online instruction can provide learning opportunities that classrooms don't, but because online education does something else. It *scales*. Technology puts a stake in the heart of the friction and barriers administrators have erected to support their premium pricing: distance. A rare holdout, higher ed's late embrace of technology could change society.

Scale will allow individual institutions—and individual professors—to exponentially expand their reach. This provides the potential to correct one of the great inequities of the last half century—the artificial scarcity of elite education. For the past ten years, my fall class has been 160 students because that's the capacity of room 2-60 in the Kaufman Management Center. This fall, unbound from the physical constraints of room 2-60, my class enrollment stands at 280. The incremental cost of almost doubling the class? I'd estimate $2,000–$3,000 (an additional graduate student instructor to handle grading).

Even as the population of qualified high school graduates has expanded, the handful of schools that hold the keys to entry into the highest-paid, most influential jobs in business, culture, and government have made the same number of keys every year. Complementing the ivory tower with an online offering allows for the mass production of those keys. And online learning, because of its flexibility, increases both the educational and profit potential of mid-career education. No sensible person would design an industry that sells its product only to eighteen- to twenty-two-year-olds when older people are looking to spend on "experiences" and to keep their skills relevant. Lifetime learning, a recurring revenue model, presents an enormous opportunity for universities to take a page from the private sector (Amazon Prime, Netflix) and evolve to a superior business model. Tech creates scale, and scale increases both access (social good) and revenue (necessary fuel).

## BAIT

Scale is also bait. It will lure the biggest predators in the jungle to an industry that has largely escaped their notice—big tech. Big tech needs to find billions of dollars in top-line revenue growth every year, and partnering with educational institutions is an obvious expansion. This will further accelerate the gap between the haves and have-nots as the elite institutions have the brand strength to attract big tech's investment in the requisite intellectual capital and technical infrastructure.

Education start-ups will attract cheap capital and seize the opportunity the pandemic has accelerated and expanded. What SARS was to ecommerce in Asia (Alibaba broke into the consumer space), Covid-19 could be to higher ed in the United States.

The rookie move is to believe that MOOCs or stand-alone education start-ups will be the big winners. (Searches for "MasterClass" have eclipsed "business school.") They won't. Why won't MasterClass be a disruptor long-term? Because MasterClass sucks. Young people don't gain value learning from celebrities, but from teachers, who can give them the skills to become celebrities.

At each university, there are 6 to 12 "ringers," great teachers who are worth it. Ringers, unbounded by the geographic constraints of their campus and parent brand, will see their compensation rise 3 to 10 times over the next decade. Administrators at the top 10 universities who have the skills to become product managers will see their comp increase. Most everyone else in traditional academia will make less.

The second-greatest accretion of stakeholder value in business, behind Amazon's entry into healthcare, will be big (and some small) tech firms partnering with world-class universities to offer 80% of a traditional four-year degree for 50% of the price. This is the gangster cocktail of the fastest-growing analog consumer brands in history (Southwest Airlines, Old Navy, etc.).

MIT and Google could jointly craft two-year degrees in STEM. The myth/magic of campuses and geography is no longer a constraining factor—most programs will be hybrid soon, dramatically increasing enrollments among the best brands. MIT/Google could enroll a hundred thousand students at $25,000 per year in tuition (a bargain), yielding $5 billion for a two-year program that would have margins rivaling . . . MIT and Google. Bocconi/Apple, Carnegie Mellon/Amazon, UCLA/Netflix, University of Washington/Microsoft . . . you get the idea.

University brands are the premier luxury brands globally, built over centuries, with margins and the illusion of scarcity that renders Hermès vulgar. If you don't own the mine (MIT), you want to sell the picks or staple tent denim to create durable pants for miners. Universities will dramatically increase their spend on technology and, in many cases, outsource entire programs (for example Duke's continuing ed). There will be enormous opportunity to substantially upgrade SaaS teaching tools, as anybody who has used Blackboard can attest.

For now, the pandemic has cleared the competitive field for virtual learning. Our current optimism notwithstanding, it will likely take longer than initially hoped before it's safe for hundreds of people to gather in crowded lecture halls, to cheer on the school basketball team, or to swarm around one another in dorm rooms and fraternity basements. In the interim, the college experience is going to be a shadow of its former self, with masks, distancing, grab-and-go food, daily temperature checks, and few of the traditional rituals and rites of passage that other generations experienced.

## TWENTY-FIRST-CENTURY HIGHER ED

When we can let all this restart, and give the on-campus experience a chance to compete with the virtual, a generation that comes of age in the pandemic may not perceive the same value in the proximity my generation cherished. By the time the virus is contained, we may have raised a micro-generation of innate distancers. Even post corona, and a return to proximity, the temporary elimination of the college experience will have catalyzed a question American households were afraid to ask: Is it worth it? After a month taking classes at home, most students were likely desperate to get back to campus. After a year without the "traditional" college experience, plenty of people will begin to wonder how much they miss it, and what it's really worth.

Moreover, the need to rethink how campuses are utilized, and the injection of online tools into the college toolbox, is going to expand the notion of the college experience. For many students, it already looks nothing like the brochures. Around 20% of college students live with their parents, and over half don't live in college housing. Twenty-seven percent of full-time students work at least 20 hours per week. In the near future, schools looking to reduce density on campus are likely to move toward rotating schedules (such as 4-to-6-week modules rather than 4-month semesters). Schools could encourage or even require students to spend a year or more away from campus, or invest in satellite campuses, as my school, NYU, has done in Dubai and Shanghai.

Finally, we cannot overlook that even for those participating in the "traditional" college experience of lecture halls and discussion sections, dorms and dining halls, there have long been inequalities and inefficiencies. Disruption is an opportunity to better serve the broader community. Women, people of color, gay and transgender students have had to fight, and still have to fight, for an equal place on our campuses. So we shouldn't be surprised that women are 50% more likely than men to say they would choose an online college option, or that Blacks are 50% more likely than whites to say they are confident in the quality of online coursework.[24] Simply put, they have less to lose, as the status quo was different for them, and as a result they stand to benefit the most from a rethinking of higher ed.

## Recommendations

What needs to happen:

- The U.S. needs a Marshall Plan to partner with states to dramatically increase the number of seats at state schools while decreasing cost for four-year universities and junior colleges. Only a third of the U.S. population has college degrees, and less than 10% have graduate degrees.

- Tax private K–12 schools to supplement public K–12 education. Higher education has become a caste system in substantial part because the rich now have a private educational system greasing the skids for entry to the best schools, and poor kids, except the truly exceptional among them, can't compete. We should be investing vastly more in our public primary and secondary schools.

- Endowments over $1 billion should be taxed if the university doesn't grow freshman seats at 1.5 times the rate of population growth. Harvard, MIT, and Yale have combined endowments (approximately $85 billion) greater than the GDP of many Latin American nations. If an organization is growing cash at a faster rate than the value they are providing, they aren't a non-profit, but a private enterprise. Senator Elizabeth Warren taught in the mother of all wine caves—Harvard.

- A dean of a top-10 school needs to be a class traitor and reevaluate tenure so as to limit it to cases where it's truly needed to secure academic freedom, rather than the expensive and innovation-killing employment perk it has become. This would require greater comp in the short run to attract world-class academics, but productivity would skyrocket, as academics would find that the market, while a harsh arbiter, often brings out great things in people when they face competition.

- We need firms (like Apple) to seize the greatest business opportunity in decades and open tuition-free universities that leverage their brand and their tech expertise to create certification programs (Apple—arts; Google—computer science; and Amazon—operations). The business model is to flip the model and charge firms to recruit (shifting costs from students to firms), bypassing the cartel that is university accreditation. Apple training, certification, testing, and reporting would lead to bidding wars among their graduates—the secret sauce for any university. I first wrote about this in 2017,[25] and one of the silver linings of the pandemic has been Google announcing, in August 2020, that the company will offer courses awarding career certificates that it and other participating employers will consider equivalent to a four-year degree in that area.[26]

- Gap years should be the norm, not the exception. An increasingly ugly secret of campus life is that a mix of helicopter parenting and social media has rendered many 18-year-olds unfit for college. Ninety percent of kids who defer and take a gap year return to college and are more likely to graduate, with better grades.

- We need national service programs. I talk more about this in chapter 5, but in brief, we should start with the

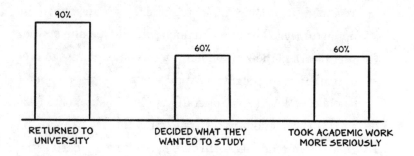

## AFTER TAKING A GAP YEAR, STUDENTS...

90%

60%                        60%

RETURNED TO          DECIDED WHAT THEY          TOOK ACADEMIC WORK
UNIVERSITY           WANTED TO STUDY            MORE SERIOUSLY

SOURCE: YEAR OUT GROUP.ORG.

Corona Corps and expand from there. National service programs of all kinds, from military to education, provide exceptional returns on investment for both the nation and those who serve.[27]

- We fetishize a university degree, but for many it's prohibitively expensive and unnecessary. A two-year community college degree in business management, marketing, or similar field is a sufficient prerequisite for many office jobs. Computer programming, UX/UI, and product management are hot fields that will get hotter, and certification programs including General Assembly and Lambda School are a gangster way of preparing a person of any age for a career in those fields in a matter of months. Many front-end developers are also self-taught through Khan Academy, YouTube, and other free resources.

- Expanding the variety and efficiency of certification programs can not only retrain workers in dying industries, but can position a young person for a rewarding entrepreneurial career. We need a nationwide vocational training system in the U.S., similar to programs in Germany, where four times more people per capita have vocational training than in the U.S. With a shifting economic and labor landscape, vocational programs could provide a changing workforce with options and purpose. Our declining life expectancy is mostly due to deaths of despair (drugs, alcohol, suicide). Many of them could be prevented if people are given dignified work options through affordable, focused training.[28]

One thing we should *not* do? Free college. That's a populist slogan and a bad idea. It's a further transfer of wealth from the poor to the rich. Only 32% of Americans go to college, and cost is not what keeps the most exceptional kids of any income level from getting to college. Improve K–12 education, strengthen two-year programs, expand the seats at the best universities, and college becomes an engine of upward mobility—without leaving behind the two thirds of people whom (better) high school serves well. College needs to be more affordable, but we don't need to subsidize the wealthiest households in America, who send 88% of their children to college.

# THE COMMONWEALTH

The pandemic has laid bare a generation's worth of poor choices and accelerated the consequences. The song remains the same: the rich get richer. The cost of a few garnering most of the gains is not just economic, it attacks the ballast of the U.S., our middle class.

For forty years, we have engaged in a gross idolatry of private enterprise and the wealth it creates, while hollowing out government institutions and denigrating public servants. When the virus hit our shores, it found a society optimized for spread. Relative to our wealth and power, America's handling of the challenge of this generation has been the worst in the world. In truth, we were sick already, riddled with comorbidities. Government agencies were weakened and science discredited. Individualism had become prized above all, resulting in a false conflation of freedom with a lack of civic duty and a refusal to bear minor inconvenience. Our muscles of collective sacrifice had atrophied so as to become feeble.

The prescription for the pandemic is the same as the prescription for our broader illness—a wholesale renewal of our sense of community. We must wrest our government from the hands of the shareholder class, which has co-opted it, and end the cronyism they have instituted to protect their wealth. We must set aside our idolatry of innovators and look unflinchingly at the exploitation it promotes. In short, we need to take government seriously—as a respectable, necessary, and noble institution—so that we can return to taking capitalism seriously, as a vibrant, sometimes harsh, but productive system that betters lives.

## Capitalism, Our Comorbidities, and the Coronavirus

Capitalism has no equal as a system for economic productivity. It yokes our natural self-interest to the profit incentive, directing our creativity and our discipline toward maximizing economic return. It puts us in competition with one another to (remarkably) generate more choice and opportunity for each of us. The market near my house offers two dozen kinds of blue cheese, fifty craft beers, and three hundred varieties of wine. Ten times that is available on my phone. From my local airport,

I can take a trip to the mountains of Colorado, the museums of Paris, or the beaches of Brazil, and be home in time to go back to work on Monday. My father in San Diego can video chat with his grandsons in Florida with the phone in his pocket (he doesn't), and then pull up every novel ever written and every film ever made on that same phone. There's even a pill to stop hair loss—little late. It's an incredible life, and the spoils of success are worth working hard for. And that hard work stokes increased competition, generating more spoils, then more competition, and so on, and so on.

The chance to participate in a system that rewards smarts and hard work is a beacon for industrious and ambitious people globally. In Depression-era Scotland, my dad was physically abused by his father. His mother spent the money he sent home from the Royal Navy on whiskey and cigarettes. So, my father took a huge risk and came to America. My mom took a similar risk, leaving her two youngest siblings in an orphanage (her parents died in their fifties), and bought a ticket on a steamship. She had a small suitcase and 110 quid that she hid in both socks. Why? Because they wanted to work their asses off and apply that work to the greatest platform in history, America. They adopted American norms (hard work, risk taking, consumption, and divorce) and provided their son with the opportunity to teach 4,700 young adults, pay tens of millions in taxes, and create hundreds of jobs (#boasting).

That's the trick of capitalism. By directing our ambition and our energy toward productive labor, it turns selfishness into wealth and stakeholder value. And ultimately, the wealth it creates becomes the spoils needed for productive altruism. On airplanes, we are told to put our own oxygen mask on before we assist someone else with theirs. That captures capitalism— get your own first, and put yourself in a position to help others. It's selfishness that ultimately benefits others as well.

Capitalism leverages our species' superpower: cooperation. In *Sapiens*, Yuval Noah Harari explains that unlike other species who can also cooperate (bees, apes, wolves), homo sapiens can cooperate *at scale*, "in extremely flexible ways with countless numbers of strangers. That's why sapiens rule the world."[1] Though our motivations may be selfish, the bounties of capitalism are the product of coordinated effort across time and space by thousands, even millions of people. In early capitalist societies, machines and factories allowed dozens, then hundreds of people to combine their efforts into one unified force. Wealth creation accelerated to rates unknown in human history.

Today, we have the corporation. Unlike a factory, the corporation is an intangible, something that exists only in our minds and a Delaware court. Yet it has extraordinary power. It combines the physical labor of thousands of people with their organizational skill, insights, and ideas. When people coordinate efforts, the whole is vastly greater than the sum of the parts. The capitalist U.S. corporation is the most productive generator of economic wealth in history.

## SOUNDS GREAT, BUT . . .

There are costs and risks to a system built on selfishness. Capitalism, despite what we have been told since the Reagan years, is not a self-regulating system. It doesn't make people virtuous, or necessarily reward virtue. Professor Harari tempers his observation that cooperation permits sapiens to "rule the world" with the recognition that our next-of-kin chimps, also capable of cooperation, but not at mass scale, "are locked up in zoos and research laboratories."

Capitalism in itself has no moral compass. The problems of unfettered capitalism are all around us. There are externalities: costs (or benefits) of activity that are not borne by an actor. Pollution is the paradigmatic externality. Acting purely for its profit-seeking self-interest, General Motors would pour the toxic waste it creates into the river behind the factory. That would mean less-expensive cars, but dire consequences for those who live and work downriver. That's not to demonize GM. If it doesn't get rid of waste in the cheapest possible way, its competition will, putting GM out of business with cheaper cars. Marx called this "the coercive law of competition," and it has no exceptions for Good Samaritans.

And there are the problems of inequality. Employers, landowners, the wealthy, the monopolist all have substantial advantages over those they employ or compete with. That's a natural and necessary aspect of capitalism, whose basic premise is that winners are rewarded and losers punished. Allowed to extend too far, however, those advantages lead to exploitation, dynasties, and the suppression of competition. Inequality is not in itself immoral, but persistent inequality is.

We don't have to imagine this—the evidence is embedded in our society. Two hundred years ago we built an economy on Black slave labor. Today Black families have on average one tenth the wealth of white families.[2] As we've noted, at many of our elite schools—passports to a better life—more students come from the top 1% of income families than from the bottom 60%.[3] Research suggests that the most important factor determining an American's life expectancy is the zip code they are born into.[4]

## THE ROLE OF GOVERNMENT

As a society, we recognize that the long-term effects of these behaviors will impoverish all of us. Dead rivers eliminate fisheries, ruin farms, and poison our bodies. Class barriers prevent the best and the brightest from each generation rising to its fullest potential, thus denying all of us of the fruits of their labor. So we cooperate (we use our superpower) and create counterweights to an unchecked market: government.

Government's charge is to stop GM from pouring toxic waste into the river. Indeed, by outlawing the wanton disposal of toxic waste, we *allow* GM to process waste in a more enlightened fashion, because we remove the threat that its competitor will take the cheaper route. We encourage GM to think critically about how it could redesign its processes to produce less waste. And we encourage entrepreneurs to start waste-processing companies, to develop new waste reduction and processing businesses. And we get cleaner, safer water, the benefits of which enrich everyone, including GM's customers.

Likewise, it's through government that we ensure the winners don't rig the system in their favor. We regulate monopolies, or break them up, so that competition can flourish. We tax the winners to invest in the common good (education, transportation, pure research) and to defend against common threats (police and fire, military, natural disasters, disease). We build out a social safety net so that when corporations fail—a necessary part of the system—the mothers and fathers who worked for them can feed their families.

The libertarian argument, which is popular in tech today, is that this form of regulation and redistribution is inefficient, that left to its own devices the market will regulate itself. If people value clean rivers, the argument goes, they won't buy cars from companies that pollute. But history and human nature show that this does not work. On a case-by-case basis, people will almost always take the cheaper alternative. Nobody wants to see children working eighteen hours a day in a clothing factory, but at the H&M outlet, the $10 T-shirt is an unmissable bargain. Consumer purchases are purposefully difficult to reverse engineer to bad actors. Nobody wants to die in a hotel fire, but after a long day of meetings, we aren't going to inspect the sprinkler system before checking in.

As a species, we are not very good at *attribution*—connecting our individual actions with the broader world or thinking long term. As consumers, we use our fast thinking.[5] So, we need government to slow our thinking, consider the long term, and register moral and principled concerns. Keeping these forces in balance—the productive energy of capitalism and the communal concerns of government—is key to long-term prosperity.

## COMORBIDITIES

In January 2020, that balance was put to an unexpected but entirely predictable test. That we failed the test so spectacularly may have been unexpected, but it too was entirely predictable. Like the virus itself, the pandemic hit hardest where its victims have comorbidities. The pandemic has laid bare and accelerated the myriad mistakes we've been making for a generation.

In the name of cutting taxes, we have defunded government's ability to serve the community. Disease kills far more people than war—we spend over $3 *trillion* treating people with chronic disease every year.[6] Yet in 2019, the Centers for Disease Control and Prevention's budget was just over $7 billion.[7] That's less than we spend on the military in four days. In January 2020, the neutered government agency that is supposed to protect us from global pandemics couldn't develop an accurate coronavirus test.

## ABANDONED

In a perverted expression of our exceptionalism, we've abandoned international cooperation and institutions. When the coronavirus first broke out in China, neither the WHO nor the CDC had sufficient staff on the ground to investigate the outbreak or coordinate with Chinese authorities. When it broke containment and spread to Europe, we shut down our borders and looked for scapegoats, even though the virus was already burning through the homeland, undetected by insufficient testing.

In the name of capitalism, we have allowed the wealthiest to enjoy returns on their capital that go untaxed, and have insulated those winnings from risk. As the pandemic tore through our economy, we poured money by the hundreds of billions into the coffers of big and small corporations, where it quickly found its way *not* onto the dinner table of those without work or sick from the virus, but into the bank accounts of the shareholder class. The result has been staggering unemployment, business closures, and economic instability the true cost of which will take years to play out. Meanwhile, the dirty secret of this pandemic, what we aren't supposed to say out loud, is that the top 10% are living their best lives. Just by virtue of stock ownership, the wealthy are *making trillions* off the pandemic as the market touches all-time highs. The market reflects our belief that, post corona, the biggest, most successful firms (publicly traded firms) will survive, consolidate the market, and emerge stronger.

In the name of individualism, many Americans have refused to follow the call for sacrifice, from serious actions like canceling events and closing businesses, to the most trivial, including wearing a mask. If you want a symbol for how broken our conception of community and patriotism has become, it is in the politicization of masks. In the name of patriotism—a value rooted in shared sacrifice—millions of Americans have refused to engage in even this minor personal inconvenience. Refusing because it comes at the request of government, which we perceive not as the embodiment of our better instincts and the guardian of our future, but as an impediment to our desires, an oppressive force to be scorned and treated as fodder for our entertainment.

For years, we built up a notion of American exceptionalism that asserts that we don't need a functioning government, that we don't need to make sacrifices, that we don't need to invest in our communities or in our future, that we don't need to cooperate with other nations, and we are somehow immune from the threats that fell upon the rest of the world. By January 2020, we had built a society, America, perfectly designed for the spread and acceleration of a pandemic—the manifestation of our exceptionalism was no longer a robust and nimble government, but a belief that our exceptionalism itself would be an immunity.

How did we get here? How did we become so arrogant?

## Capitalism on the Way Up,
## Socialism on the Way Down = Cronyism

The logical alternative to capitalism is socialism, and on its face, there is a lot to like. Socialism is rooted in altruism and humanism; it seeks to build up community rather than the atomized individual. These are noble goals. But the sacrifice in productivity is immense, especially with the compounding effects of time. Capitalism creates dramatically many more spoils, so any empathy has more to work with.

The toxic cocktail, however, is to combine the worst of both systems. For the last forty years, we've been doing this in the United States. We have capitalism on the way up. If you can create value in this country, you can be rewarded with spoils vastly beyond anything comparable in history. If you can't create value, if you're born into the wrong family or you catch a bad break—you'll likely live on the edge and pay dearly for your mistakes. A Hunger Games economy.

Should you reach the heights of wealth (or more likely, be born into them), circumstances change. Despite our rhetoric about personal responsibility and freedom, we've embraced socialism—at the top and on the way down. We don't tolerate failure here in our socialist paradise. Rather than let companies fail—a defining and essential feature of capitalism—we have bailouts. But bailouts are hate crimes against future generations, sticking our children and grandchildren with the resulting debt.

Crisis after crisis, our rationales vary: After 9/11 it was national security. In 2008 it was liquidity, and in 2020 it was protecting the vulnerable. But our response is always the same. Protect the shareholder class, protect the executive class. Keep these firms on life support so their owners and managers don't suffer. Pay for it with debt, a burden to be borne by middle-class taxpayers and, ultimately, by our children. However, history tells us, nearly every bailout, whether it's Chrysler or Long-Term Capital Management, only creates moral hazard that results in a bigger failure and a more costly bailout. Our $1.5 billion bailout of Chrysler in 1979 graduated to a $12.5 billion bailout, bankruptcy, and a sale to Fiat in 2009. The Federal Reserve's 1998 intervention in the LTCM debacle gave Wall Street banks the confidence to take on even riskier strategies, with far greater consequences that would emerge a decade later. Every time, we're told "this is different, historic . . . and requires intervention" and that taxpayers should bail out shareholders.

But so too is an 11-year bull market a historical event. *That* was the unique event that accrued unprecedented wealth to a fraction of the population. And the corporations that benefited didn't save for a rainy day (which always comes), or pay it out to their workers so they could build up a protective cushion of wealth, or invest in capital projects that would grow the economy. Instead they poured it into dividends and stock buybacks, juicing executive compensation (from 2017 to 2019 the CEOs of Delta, American, United, and Carnival Cruises earned over

$150 million in total compensation) and shareholder returns. Since 2000, U.S. airlines have declared bankruptcy 66 times. Despite the obvious vulnerability of the sector, boards and CEOs of the six largest airlines have spent 96% of their free cash flow on share buybacks. That bolstered the share price and compensation of management, but left these companies dangerously exposed to a crisis.

Now that the crisis is upon us, this small population of rich people has found socialism, and they have their hand out. That hand should go back in their damn pocket.

## THE VIRTUES OF FAILURE

Failure, and its consequences, is a necessary part of the system. Economic dislocation and crises have real costs, but they are also opportunities for renewal. Old relationships are severed, assets are freed up, and innovation demanded. A forest fire brings life as it destroys—so too, economic upheavals create light and air for innovation to flourish. The 1918 influenza epidemic was devastating, but it was followed by the Roaring Twenties. The strongest businesses are those that are started in lean times. Wages rise after disruptions like pandemics—*if* the natural cycles of disruption and renewal are allowed to function.

We've let ourselves confuse corporations with the things they own and the people they employ. Corporations are simply abstractions. They feed nobody, house nobody, educate nobody. When a corporation fails, those who have risked their capital to

## RESPONSE OF REAL WAGES IN EUROPE FOLLOWING PREVIOUS PANDEMICS
### AMONG 12 GLOBAL PANDEMICS WITH >100K DEATHS

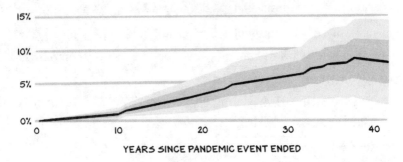

YEARS SINCE PANDEMIC EVENT ENDED

SOURCE: "LONGER-RUN ECONOMIC CONSEQUENCES OF PANDEMICS," UC DAVIS, MARCH 2020.

support it lose their investment, but the workers are still capable of work, the assets remain available, and whatever need the corporation was filling remains.

As long as we keep making old people and younger people want to take their kids to Disney's Galaxy's Edge, there will be cruise lines and airlines. Let Carnival and Delta go into Chapter 11, and ships and planes will continue to float and fly, and there will still be a steel tube with recirculated air waiting for you post molestation by Roy from TSA.

Letting firms fail and share prices fall to their market level also provides younger generations with the same opportunities we, Gen X and boomers, were given: a chance to buy Amazon at 50 (vs. 100) times earnings and Brooklyn real estate at $300 (vs. $1,500) per square foot. As Thomas Piketty has pointed out, the high growth recoveries that follow economic shocks are periods of real wage growth, whereas slow and steady growth tends to favor the wealthy.

Once the government gets into the business of propping up the losers, you can predict who will be first in line for the handouts: the people with the most political power—corporations and rich people. It's not just a matter of their lobbyists and their lawyers and their press flacks, though that's a big leg up. There's also something more insidious: cronyism.

## MY DINNER WITH DARA

Why "cronyism"? I write about tech executives, but I mostly refuse to meet with them. In part because I'm an introvert and don't enjoy meeting new people. But also because intimacy is a function of contact. Often when I meet someone, I like them as a person, feel empathy for them, and find it harder to be objective about their actions. Most senior people at successful companies are very smart, involved in interesting work, privy to inside baseball, and got where they are in part because they are good with people. I'm sure if I met more of them, I'd like them. That's why I don't meet with them. As Malcom Gladwell points out, the people who did *not* meet Hitler got him right. Easy to be charmed, even by someone so macabre, when meeting in person.

Not long ago I was invited to an "intimate" dinner with Dara Khosrowshahi, the CEO of Uber. His PR team was looking to spread Vaseline over the lens of exploitation that Uber levies daily on its 4 million "driver partners." I turned it down. I met

Dara once, years ago, when he was at Travelocity and I was pitching them on a company I'd started. He struck me as sharp and personable. I'm sure if I had gone to that dinner, I'd like him even more. And the more I got to know Dara, the more I'd like him, and the more I'd see Uber not as a legal fiction subject to the harsh law of the market, but as Dara's company, imbued with Dara's good traits.

I wish politicians would adopt a similar policy. It's difficult for our elected leaders not to shape public policy around the concerns and priorities of the superwealthy when the wealthy few have much more access. It's easiest to identify with those who are most like us and those we spend the most time with. It's our tribal nature. But this sort of access is embedded in our system. And it goes well beyond orchestrated events like my dinner with Dara. The median wealth of Democratic senators is $946,000, Republican senators $1.4 million. They send their kids to expensive schools, they eat at expensive restaurants, they go on elite vacations. The people they see all around them are Uber executives, not Uber drivers. It's only natural that they give Uber executives the benefit of the doubt, and have trouble focusing their attention on Uber drivers.

## CRONIES GONNA CRONY

The federal government's response to the pandemic has been true to form. Under the cloud cover of "protecting the most vulnerable," we've handed trillions of dollars to the most powerful.

The $2-trillion relief package passed in March 2020 was a theft from future generations. Personal income was 7.3% higher in Q2 versus Q1 of 2020 because of stimulus payments and extra unemployment benefits. The personal savings rate hit a historic 33% in April, the highest by far since the department started tracking in the 1960s. The relief package included a $90 billion tax cut that benefited almost exclusively people making over $1 million per year.[8] The richer you were, the more you gained. At the beginning of August, U.S. billionaires had increased their wealth a total of $637 billion.[9] It appears, as has been the case for decades, that the only bipartisan action is reckless spending that benefits rich people while throwing some funds at the neediest for optics.

Not every dollar will be wasted. Maybe a third of it will go to the needy. A few local restaurants will be able to pay their employees and reopen when the pandemic recedes. A firm that provides airplane maintenance, a brand strategy firm, a locksmith—they could not have planned for the pandemic and will resume paying taxes and providing a service post corona. Those successes will be held up as evidence of the value of the bailout.

Except that the majority of the money we are asking our children to repay has done nothing but flatten the curve for rich people. Rich people have registered disproportionate benefit, their preexisting relationships with banks getting them to the front of the line. Look no further than the refusal of the administration to reveal who is getting the money—until after the election, of course.[10]

Instead of letting market failures play out, we propped up the shareholder class, using money stolen from the next generation. "We're all in this together," they tell us. Bullshit. The really ugly truth is this: for the wealthy, the pandemic means less commuting and emissions, more time with family, and more wealth (see above: markets at all-time highs).

## Cronyism and Inequality

The obscene $2.2 trillion Covid relief package was just a symptom of our cronyism. The systemic flaw is that our government is no longer keeping capitalism's winners in check. Instead, it's a coconspirator in their entrenchment.

The wealthy have done well over the past few decades, in a supernova kind of way. A ton has been written on this, because the data is abundant. There is shocking data at the extremes: the top 0.1% now own more of the nation's wealth than the bottom 80%.[11] The three richest Americans hold more wealth than the bottom 50%. And there is bad news in broad strokes as well: since 1983, the share of national wealth owned by lower- and middle-income families has declined from 39% of the pie to 21%, while upper-income families have increased their share of national wealth from 60% to 79%.

For purposes of self-preservation, you'd think the rich would be concerned with this level of income inequality. At some point, the bottom half of the globe by income realizes they can double their wealth by taking the wealth of the richest

# SHARE OF U.S. AGGREGATE WEALTH

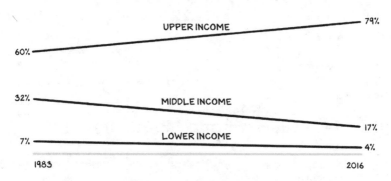

UPPER INCOME — 79%

60%

32% — MIDDLE INCOME

7% — LOWER INCOME — 17%
4%

1983                    2016

SOURCE: PEW RESEARCH CENTER ANALYSIS OF THE SURVEY OF CONSUMER FINANCES.

8 families, who have more money than 3.6 billion people. Here in the U.S. the bottom 25% of households (31 million families) have a median net worth of $200.[12] Most recently, a group of protesters built a guillotine outside the Manhattan home of Jeff Bezos to commemorate his wealth passing $200 billion.

This trend is only getting worse. Once, we elected leaders who cut the tops of trees to ensure saplings get sunlight. Today there is less and less sunlight. A recent study of historical tax-return data concluded that the uber-wealthy paid a tax rate of 70% in the fifties, 47% in the eighties, and 23% at present—a lower tax rate than the middle class. Whereas poor and middle-class tax rates have largely stayed the same.

We've exploded the debt so rich people pay less tax. Money is the transfer of work and time, and we've decided our kids will need to work more in the future, and spend less time with their families, so wealthy people can pay lower taxes today.

## TOTAL TAX RATE BY INCOME PERCENTILE (FEDERAL, STATE, AND LOCAL)
1950–2018

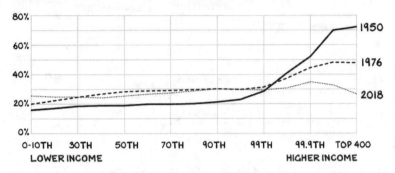

SOURCE: EMMANUEL SAEZ & GABRIEL ZUCMAN, UC BERKELEY.

My own experience provides a case study in how the wealthy lock in their gains. When I sold my last company, L2, in 2017, I paid an effective tax rate of 17–18%. I paid 22.8% federal, but the first $10 million were tax free, thanks to Section 1202 of the tax code. Section 1202 is a tax break for early shareholders, meant to encourage start-ups. Only it's nothing but a transfer of wealth from other taxpayers to venture capitalists and founders. No entrepreneur starts, or doesn't start, a business because of the tax code. It takes a special kind of crazy to start a company and a lot of talent, work, and luck to build it to be something you can sell for millions of dollars. The decision has nothing to do with the tax code. Tax breaks for the successful are just another way we deepen inequality.

Once people make the jump to light speed, advantages like this let them pull away. Access to more resources, investment opportunities, lower taxes, tax specialists, political contacts, friends who can help your kid get into school, and the wheel spins. It's never been easier to become a billionaire, or harder to become a millionaire.

## ECONOMIC ANXIETY

Proponents of unfettered capitalism shrug off the ever-increasing advantages of the wealthy and trust a rising tide lifts all boats. They rest easy knowing that working-class Americans may not have secured the same portion of our recent prosperity, but their lives are nonetheless better than they were a decade, a generation, or a century ago. This profoundly misunderstands the nature of economic security.

In 2018, 106 million Americans lived below twice the federal poverty line, which is not as nice as it sounds. Twice the poverty level for a family of four is a household income of $51,583.[13] That population has increased at twice the rate of the population as a whole since 2000. Most of them spend more than one third of their income on rent. A third do not have health insurance, despite being disproportionately sick or disabled.[14] Many carry the burden of unmanageable debt, which can lead to deaths of despair. People who take their own life are eight times more likely than average to be in debt.[15] For every 100 points your credit score increases, your risk of dying in the next three months declines by 4.4%.[16] In the U.S., money is literally life.

Economic anxiety was the sound track of my childhood—a

static noise in the background. We were never well off, and after my parents' divorce, economic stress turned to economic anxiety. It gnawed at my mom and me, whispering in our ears that we weren't worthy, that we'd failed. Our household income was $800 a month when my parents split. My mom, a secretary, was smart and hardworking. Soon, our income increased to $900 a month, as she got not one but two raises—the munitions in the battle of me and her against the world. I told my mom, at the age of nine, that I didn't need a babysitter, as I knew we could use the additional $8 a week. Also my sitter was a religious freak who, when the ice-cream truck came by, gave each of her kids 30 cents and me 15.

The winter of my ninth year, I had no suitable jacket, so off to Sears we went. The jacket cost $33, nearly a day's pay for my mom, I knew. We bought a size too big, as my mom figured I could go two, maybe three years with this jacket. What she hadn't counted on was that her son loses things. All the time.

Two weeks later, I left the jacket at my Boy Scouts meeting, but I assured my mom we'd get it back at the next meeting. We didn't. So, off to JCPenney to get another jacket. This time my mom told me the jacket was my Christmas present, as we couldn't afford gifts after buying another jacket. I don't know if this was true or if she was trying to teach me a lesson. Likely both. Regardless, I tried to feign excitement at my early Christmas present. A few weeks later, though, I . . . lost the jacket.

That day, I sat at home after school, waiting for my mom

to come home, feeling the body blow I had delivered to our economically distressed household. Yes, it was just a lost jacket, but I was nine. And the point is not that I had a hard life—I didn't, by any reasonable measure. The point is that it was *just a jacket*. But my sense of economic anxiety was already so finely tuned that the loss of a jacket was chilling. I will never forget that feeling of dread and self-loathing I felt that day.

"I lost the jacket," I told her. "It's okay, I don't need one . . . I swear." I felt like crying, bawling really. However, something worse happened. My mom began to cry, composed herself, walked over to me, made a fist and pounded on my thigh several times. As if she were in a boardroom trying to make a point, and my thigh was the table she was slamming her fist on. I don't know if it was more upsetting or awkward. She then went upstairs to her room, came down an hour later, and we never spoke of it again.

I still lose things. Sunglasses, credit cards, hotel room keys. I don't even carry house keys, why bother? The difference is that, now, it's an inconvenience, quickly addressed. Wealth cushions the small blows—lost jacket, an overlooked electric bill, a flat tire—while insecurity magnifies them. Economic anxiety is similar to high blood pressure. Always there, waiting to turn a minor ailment into a life-threatening disease. Indeed, it's literally high blood pressure: kids who live in low-income households have higher resting blood pressure than kids who live in wealthy households.[17]

# The New Caste System

It's not novel to point out that it's good to be rich, or that it's bad to be poor. Perhaps the ambition and drive that powers capitalism needs the spur of poverty to keep it moving. But the fundamental promise of America, of any just society, is that with hard work and talent, anyone can lift themselves up, up out of poverty, up into prosperity. And that promise has been broken.

Study after study has found that in today's America, the biggest determinant of an individual's economic success is not talent, it's not hard work, and it's not even luck. It's how much money their parents have. The expected family income of children raised in families at the 90th income percentile is three times that of children raised at the 10th.[18] Economic mobility in the United States, on a range of measures, is worse, in many cases much worse, than in Europe and elsewhere.[19] Want to live the American dream? Move to Denmark.[20]

This isn't just a story about the poor or billionaires. At every level, it's getting harder and harder to move up. My first house in the Potrero Hill neighborhood of San Francisco was $280,000. Divide that by the $100,000 average starting salary out of business school in 1992 and you end up with a ratio of 2.8 for the price of housing compared to average salary. Now the average salary is $140,000. That's a lot of money. But the average home in the Bay Area now costs $1.4 million. So, we've gone from a ratio of 2.8 to a ratio of 10. This is for the nominal winners, the people who thought they were joining the elite. It's harder now.

The result is a society in which there is tremendous prosperity, but little progress. The Declaration of Independence promises us "life, liberty, and the pursuit of happiness." Yet study after study finds that Americans live shorter lives,[21] are less free,[22] and less successful in our pursuit of happiness[23] than our European counterparts.

## PRIVATE DISNEYLAND

These inequalities are rooted in the tax code, our education system, and our woeful social services. Now they are embedding themselves in our culture.

When I went to Disneyland when I was a kid, there were rich kids, middle-income kids, and lower-income kids. My best friend was a Mormon kid going to Stanford. My other friend, from a wealthy family, was going to Brown. And my other friend, a Black kid from the inner city who had no money, was trying to go to a mediocre college in Oregon on a football scholarship. And we all experienced the same Disneyland. We all paid $9.50 for our ticket books. We all hoarded our "E" tickets and waited 45 minutes in line for the Pirates of the Caribbean. We all had a similar experience at Disney.

Now Disney says, for those of you who don't have a lot of money, it's $119. You eat mediocre food, and you wait in line. For those of you who are a little wealthier, you can pay $170 and get something called a FastPass. And instead of waiting an hour for the Pirates of the Caribbean, you only wait ten minutes. And for those of you in the 1%, you can do a VIP tour. For $5,000 you and six friends get a tour guide, lunch in a special dining room served by costumed characters, backstage access, and not only do you get to cut the line, you go through an employee entrance.

## ON EDUCATION, AGAIN

Okay, but Disneyland was never supposed to be a communist utopia. It's free enterprise, right? Perhaps, although I'd argue that making rich kids wait in line at Disneyland probably had some salutary effects on their altruism, sense of empathy, and ability to handle irritations. But if Disneyland adopting a caste system doesn't bother you, consider this. Read that passage again, only replace every mention of "Disneyland" with "college." It's the same. Higher education was supposed to be the great uplifter, the antidote to capitalism's tendency toward classism. But higher education in the U.S. has morphed from the lubricant of upward mobility to the *enforcer* of our caste system.

What changed my circumstances from crying over a lost jacket, to laughing when my son loses his ("just like your dad"), was the University of California. When I graduated high school (with a 3.2 GPA), the acceptance rate at UCLA was over 60%. I still didn't get in on my first try, but an empowered admissions official took pity on my appeal. That moment of grace, and the generosity of California taxpayers that made it possible, has been the foundation of my success. From UCLA I secured a job on Wall Street, and then admission to UC Berkeley's business school. I met my first wife at UCLA (still friends), and it was her income that gave me the flexibility to cofound Prophet and Red Envelope. I met my business partner at Berkeley, and without him neither of those companies would have made it out of my head. One of my professors at Berkeley, David Aaker, became a mentor, and his association with Prophet opened the early doors that enabled our early success.

More than any other single factor, it's access to higher education that has been the secret to my success. The firms we've started have generated over a quarter of a billion dollars for investors, employees, and the founders. These firms employ hundreds of people—and neither of my parents went to college, but America wanted their kid to attend. Yet as I detailed in chapter 4, that path out of economic anxiety is getting steeper and narrower. In 2019, the acceptance rate at UCLA was 12%. Put another way, it's five times as difficult to access the upward mobility that was within reach three decades ago. A rich society should make it easier for the next generation to get ahead, not harder. A privileged few are riding the Pirates of the Caribbean over and over, while the masses are standing outside in the sun waiting for a turn that may never come.

## WEALTH PRIVILEGE

We don't see the depth of our dilemma because we've bought into myths about America, meritocracy, and success. We've put billionaires on a pedestal and made wealth the signifier of worth—and it's to be rewarded with . . . more wealth.

Don't look to the wealthy to arrest this trend. We love being told our success is the product of our own genius. After serving on seven consumer, media, and technology public company boards, my experience is that if you tell a thirty- or fortysomething person who wears black turtlenecks that they are Steve Jobs, they are inclined to believe you.

## CARTOON

There is a cartoon that very wealthy people are generally assholes. They are not. My experience is that most very successful people have a few things in common: grit, luck, talent, and a tolerance for risk. Sure, there are rich kids, but in general this cohort may be the hardest-working cohort of any segment. They receive more return (economic and non-economic), so there are greater incentives, but there's no escaping it—if you're planning on being a billionaire (and don't have billionaire parents), you should plan on working for the next 30 years . . . and not much else. I'm not pushing hustle porn—the jobs that create multimillionaires are just extremely demanding. I've also found that most of the superwealthy are patriotic, generous, and genuinely concerned about the commonwealth. That makes sense, as to reach the pinnacle of success, it helps to have people pulling for you.

But wealthy people are not going to disarm unilaterally. Like anyone else, the 0.1% will use their skills and resources to ensure their firm has an advantage over others, that their children have an advantage over others, even if that means turning a blind eye to externalities (environmental standards, monopoly abuse, tax avoidance, teen depression). We all want the best for our kids, and our system gives us the option to buy a better education, to pay for better cultural development, and to provide more opportunity for our offspring. Most everyone cares about the long-term health of our society, but first we focus on ourselves and our own.

Conflating luck and talent is dangerous. The Pareto principle posits that even if competence is evenly distributed, 80% of effects stem from 20% of the causes. As I get older, I'm struck by how big a part luck played in my life—being born in the right place at the right time—and how much I mistook it for skill. Coming of professional age as a white male in the 1990s was the greatest economic arbitrage in history. Today's 54-to-70-year-olds saw the Dow Jones increase an average of 445% from 25–40, their prime working years. For other ages, it doubles at most.

That growth meant more opportunities—opportunities that were sequestered to a specific demographic (see above: white males). In 1990s San Francisco, between the age of 34 and 44, I raised over $1 billion for my start-ups and activist campaigns. I didn't know a single woman, or person of color, under 40 who raised more than $10 million.

And it seemed normal. Even today, white men hold 65% of elected offices despite being 31% of the population.[24] Eighty percent of venture capitalists—the gatekeepers of the entrepreneurial economy—are men, and most of them are white. Is it any wonder that founder-CEOs, from Bill and Steve to Bezos and Zuck, are overwhelmingly white men too?

## SHARE OF VENTURE CAPITALISTS
2018

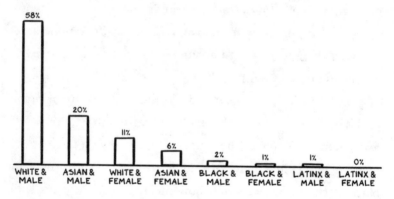

SOURCE: RICHARD KERBY.

The difficult thing about a meritocracy—or what we think is a meritocracy—is that we believe billionaires deserve it and that we should idolize them. Our idolatry of innovators blinds the winners to the structural advantages and luck they benefited from. And it fools us into thinking we are just a few lucky breaks from joining them. Sixty percent of Americans believe the economic system unfairly favors the wealthy[25]—but, as John

Oliver points out, we tolerate this, because we think, "I can clearly see this game is rigged, which is what will make it so sweet when I win this thing."[26] Then we wonder why veterans are urinating on Market Street and why 18% of children live in households that are food insecure.[27]

The greater our differences economically, the more we come to believe we are different in more fundamental ways. Altruistic behavior decreases in times of greater income inequality. The rich are more generous in times of lesser inequality and less generous when inequality grows more extreme. Michael Lewis writes, "The problem is caused by the inequality itself: it triggers a chemical reaction in the privileged few. It tilts their brains. It causes them to be less likely to care about anyone but themselves or to experience the moral sentiments needed to be a decent citizen."[28] Privilege looks in the mirror and sees nobility. Financially successful people come to believe that someone who is delivering groceries at $14 an hour or cleaning the subway car deserves their economic fate. They're not as smart, they're not as good, they're not as *worthy* as the rest of us.

Worse, those not blessed by circumstance and luck hear the message loud and clear. Lack of economic success is their fault. This is the land of opportunity, where anyone can make it big, right? So what does that say about those who don't?

When we put the 0.1% on a pedestal, we crowd out teachers, social workers, bus drivers, and farmworkers from the respect that is due to them. We tell them they are less, that they have failed. That any economic disadvantages they face are their fault, their birthright even. That's not capitalism, that's a caste system—and the inevitable result of cronyism, which requires these myths to entrench the power of the 0.1%.

This is why we need a strong government, to counter human nature, to balance fast thinking and selfishness with slow thinking and community. We don't need to make idols of the wealthy to inspire achievement. Wealth and success are motivation enough. We are not dressing billionaires up as heroes because they need better marketing. We are dressing them to obscure the truth—that while innovation still happens, and hard work still exists, an ever-increasing share of the spoils are not going to the innovators but to the owners.

## CORPORATIONS ARE (RICH) PEOPLE TOO

What's happening at the individual level is also happening at the corporate level. Just as we have tilted the tax code toward the shareholder class, large corporations have co-opted the government agencies that are supposed to constrain their power.

Why does this matter? It kills innovation and job growth. Nearly twice as many new companies were formed each day during the Carter administration as are formed now.[29] That tax-free $10 million hasn't birthed new companies, it's destroyed them. In markets dominated by one of the Four, early-stage venture investors are increasingly uninterested in funding an insect to splat into the windshield of a monopoly.

Unthreatened by meaningful competition, supplied with near-

## NUMBER OF SEED ROUNDS BY CATEGORY
2010-2018

COMPETES WITH FACEBOOK/GOOGLE

COMPETES WITH AMAZON

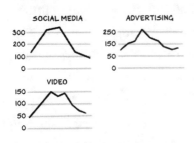

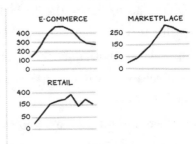

SOURCE: TOM TUNGUZ BLOG ANALYSIS.

infinite cheap capital, and enjoying the power of a flywheel to gain advantage in any industry they enter, big tech is no longer motivated to innovate. They have a much more lucrative profit opportunity: exploitation.

# The Exploitation Economy

In the past decade, we have transitioned from an innovation economy to an exploitation economy. Innovation is dangerous and unpredictable. It changes market dynamics and creates opportunities for nimble new players to steal share from established players. None of that is attractive to an entrenched market leader. Why should Apple "Think Different" when the way it's currently thinking has made its shareholders over $1 trillion dollars in the past 12 months (ending August 2020)?

The firms that have grown shareholder value by hundreds of billions in a short time have arbitraged the inability of our government, and our instincts, to keep pace with technology. On the other side of the billions of shareholder value captured by increasingly few from social media, trading, or ride-hailing apps are millions of depressed teens, election interference, and a decrease in the dignity of work (no health insurance, sub-minimum-wage compensation).

Dominant firms exploit everything they touch, starting with their own workers. The pandemic revealed Amazon's attitude toward its "essential" warehouse workers. Workers walked out, started petition drives, and made internal complaints about Covid risks and unsafe conditions. In response, Amazon . . . fired the fulfillment center worker who organized a walkout.[30]

Uber has figured out how to run a massively asset-intensive business without assets. Instead it puts the responsibility of buying and maintaining its assets on driver partners that it fights tooth and nail to avoid classifying as employees, so that it doesn't have to provide health insurance or pay minimum wage. California Assembly Bill 5 (AB5) extends employee classification status to gig workers because, well, they are employees. In response, the gig industry put together Proposition 22 for voters to decide on this November. The bill, as you might suspect, suspends AB5 and creates a new, less costly classification. The "No on 22" campaign raised $811,000, mostly from labor groups. "Yes on 22" has raised . . . $110 million.[31]

Uber's model is brilliant, and absurd. Imagine if United Airlines told flight crews that if they wanted to make that day's JFK to LAX run, they would need to finance the airplane, fuel it up, and stock it with in-flight snacks, and then get a revenue split. One might argue it's simply the franchise model. Most franchises pay 4–8% to the parent—Uber takes 20%.

If there was any doubt that Uber's business is untenable in a world where its drivers make minimum wage, it vanished in August when the company admitted that it would have to limit its business to denser urban areas if it were required to classify its "driver partners" for what they are: employees.[32]

The biggest companies are increasingly getting their profits

## BENEFITS FOR DELIVERY DRIVERS

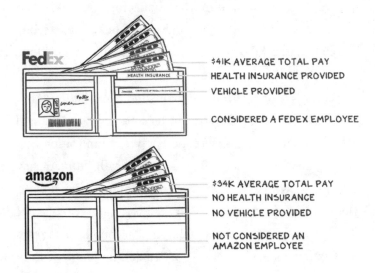

$41K AVERAGE TOTAL PAY
HEALTH INSURANCE PROVIDED
VEHICLE PROVIDED

CONSIDERED A FEDEX EMPLOYEE

$34K AVERAGE TOTAL PAY
NO HEALTH INSURANCE
NO VEHICLE PROVIDED

NOT CONSIDERED AN
AMAZON EMPLOYEE

SOURCE: GLASSDOOR.

from exploiting another fertile target—their own consumers. There's no such thing as a free social network app. Instead, companies are increasingly using algorithms to leverage our weaknesses as a species. Most disease and hardship for our species has been a function of scarcity—too little salt, sugar, fat, approval, safety, opportunities to mate. As a result, when we find these things, our brain produces the ultimate reward, the pleasure hormone dopamine. And it makes sense: Nature rewards behaviors that ensure the survival and propagation of the species.

## SUPERABUNDANCE

The assembly line, processing power, and Amazon Prime have not only met the minimum thresholds for survival but created a new threat to our species: superabundance. Diabetes, income inequality, and fake news—all are a function of our belief that more is better.

Survival, propagation, and consumption should result in a next generation that's smarter, faster, and stronger. Where things have come off the rails is a function of our innovation economy moving faster than our instincts. Historically, humans have engaged in activities that have natural stopping cues—no more apples on the tree, no more ale in the barrel, the end of a chapter, the end credits. Platforms including Facebook, Instagram, and Netflix have systematically eradicated stopping cues—similar to casinos, which deliberately have no hard angles, only one continuous space to keep you moving through it, on to the next wager. Netflix has become an endless show; TikTok, an endless video.

Technological progress lapping the calibration of our instincts culminates in endless scroll. We're unable to find the off switch. Unlike our parents and grandparents, for us dopamine release no longer depends on sacrifice, engagement, or grit, but on sitting still, as in 4, 3, 2 seconds episode 5 of *Killing Eve* will begin. There are more filtered photos, more porn, more equities, more margin, more dopa . . . more time without the nuisance of needing to engage in . . . life.

Taking away barriers is just the beginning. Adding artificial incentives, known as gamification, is what's next. The latest industry to discover this particular form of digital crack are online trading platforms (OTPs). What does endless scroll look like on a trading platform? Download Robinhood (at your own risk):

- Confetti falls to celebrate transactions
- Colorful candy crush interface
- Gamification: users can tap up to 1000 times per day to improve their position on the waitlist for Robinhood's cash management feature (essentially a high-yield checking account on the app)[33]

This discrepancy in modulation has exploded our levels of teen depression and social chaos.[34] We are in a Supermarine

Spitfire, accelerating every day, hoping the fuselage holds to-gether as we approach the sound barrier—streaming 31 seasons of *The Simpsons*, lifelike video games, ubiquitous porn of increas-ing extremes, high-def documentation in real time of the party your 15-year-old daughter wasn't invited to, social media algo-rithms fueled on outrage vs. veracity, and immediate approval of margin for a "bull put spread."

We saw the ultimate cost of this manipulation in June 2020 with the suicide of a 20-year-old from Naperville, Illinois, named Alex Kearns. Alex was interested in the markets and began trad-ing stocks on Robinhood. Then, no doubt encouraged by how easy Robinhood made it, he started trading options. Then, not understanding the complex rules of this particular crack deal, he thought he was down $730,000. Seeing no way out, Alex took his own life.

Robinhood users skew young (32% of visitors are 25–34 years old). The firm reported 3 million new accounts in Q1 2020. Half were first-time traders.[35] In addition, with Vegas and sports wa-gering all but shut down in the early months of the pandemic, OTPs have become the place where emerging gambling addic-tion can take root—a rehab facility where your sponsor is a dealer. How many of those $1,200 stimulus checks were levered up and went straight to OTPs?

The bulk of the pressure to protect kids from device addic-tion falls on parents—limiting use (severely) and getting other parents at school to limit use as well, so kids don't feel ostracized. It's difficult, and needs to be done. An "electronics fast," perhaps for the whole family, can allow the nervous system to reset. Lowering your dopamine threshold allows a smaller amount of pleasure to be satisfying.

The threat of addiction has been slowing our household down. One of our sons demonstrates behavior consistent with device addiction. It's terrifying. Everything he does, says, and works toward is in pursuit of the dopa hit waiting on his iPad. His mom and I are doing what most parents would do—reading, seeking outside help, limiting use. But more than anything, we're trying to slow things down. Time with him, especially outdoors or with books. Time in bed with him telling him stories about his grandfather becoming a frogman in the Royal Navy. Slowing everything down. It appears to be working.

I see Alex Kearns, and I see my oldest son. A nerd with a big smile, fascinated by the markets and seeking dopa hits. I can't imagine the pain of that family. I can't imagine how we've lost the script, letting the meaningful, innovation and money, trump the profound, our kids. The youth suicide rate has increased 56% in a decade.[36] Girls between 10 and 14 had a tripling of self-harm episodes between 2009 and 2015.[37] Teens who are on social media for 5+ hours a day are twice more likely to be depressed than those who are on for less than an hour.[38]

Is it any wonder Tim Cook doesn't want his nephew on social media? If he wasn't Tim Cook, would he also say, I don't want him to have an iPad either?

## MAIN REASONS FOR NEGATIVE EFFECTS OF SOCIAL MEDIA AMONG U.S. TEENS

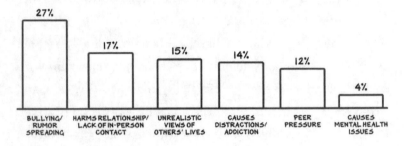

SOURCE: PEW RESEARCH CENTER, 2018.

# Take Government Seriously

I have benefited a great deal from the private markets. The freedom to follow optimism, some native talent mixed with a lot of luck, and hard work have yielded a set of professional experiences and economic security my parents wonder at, but can't fathom. At the same time, the government has given me more. The University of California was essential, as were my public primary and secondary schools. So was the rule of law that kept our businesses safe and contracts enforceable. So was the government-funded physical and digital infrastructure those businesses were built on.

Government—like private enterprise—can be inefficient and ineffective. But as Yale Law professor Daniel Markovits, author of *The Meritocracy Trap*, points out, government can also be incredibly *efficient*. A family with $60,000 annual income pays about $10,000 per year in taxes. In exchange, that family gets roads, public schools, environmental protection, national security, fire, and police—try assembling that as a package of private services and see what it costs you. That same family probably pays $3,000 a year to the Comcast Corporation for cable, internet, and mobile. Cable sucks, and the internet speeds in the U.S. are inferior to other advanced nations. In other words, government can be very efficient when we work together.[39]

Yet over the course of my lifetime, it has become fashionable to denigrate government, to deny its contributions to the commonwealth. At first, during the Reagan revolution, it was an enemy, a repressive force to be beaten. Then we stopped giving it even the respect of a worthy adversary. In 2016, the election of a reality television star as president was the fulfillment of a long-term trend. We equate government to an entertainment product. Like the NFL, but more dangerous, and year-round. We join either Team Red or Team Blue, and then we watch our teams give each other Parkinson's.

Our contempt for the government has become an investor relations strategy. On August 20, software firm Palantir sent financial documents to its investors in advance of its planned IPO. In the filing, the firm states its strong ties to government contractors were an opportunity, citing the "systemic failures of government institutions to provide for the public."[40]

"We believe that the underperformance and loss of legitimacy of many of these institutions will only increase the speed with which they are required to change," said the firm ... backed by Peter Thiel, the guy who backed Facebook, the firm that has done more than any other to contribute to that "loss of legitimacy."

Think about this. Only big tech is arrogant enough to assure investors its biggest customer will buy more because it's just so damn incompetent. Imagine Accenture telling investors it sees increased demand for its services because corporate America is just plain stupid. It's true the federal government has not demonstrated fiscal competence. In 2020, the U.S. will spend a third more than it collects ($4.8 trillion vs. $3.7 trillion).[41] However, according to its investor documents, Palantir registered losses of $580 million on $743 million in revenues, meaning it spent $1.32 billion, or *two* thirds more than it took in.

Perhaps Uncle Sam should be advising Palantir.

## YOU GET WHAT YOU PAY FOR

Our disrespect translates to our fiscal priorities, and renders our dismissal of government a self-fulfilling prophecy. We don't pay teachers enough, our schools suffer, and we lose respect for public schools. We don't pay government scientists and researchers enough (and we don't listen to the ones we do hire), and the best and the brightest go instead to Google or Amazon. Then we ask the DOJ and the FTC to restrain these corporate titans, but we tie their hands, allocating a fraction of the resources private companies deploy. Amazon has more full-time lobbyists in DC than there are sitting U.S. senators.

## TEST KITS

The pandemic has feasted on our disrespect. The wealthiest country in history, and we couldn't produce a working coronavirus test kit for months. Government scientists were sidelined, and partisanship swamped sense. Team Blue hates Team Red because they are putting grandparents in danger by not wearing masks. Team Red hates Team Blue because they are infringing on liberty and threatening the economy over something that hasn't impacted anyone they know. Then, once the virus overwhelmed us, we concocted a flawed economic bailout program. Red-state governors and blue university chancellors opted for politics and money over the health of the country and reopened prematurely.

## ON THE KINDNESS OF BILLIONAIRES

If we want a better government, we should stop sending eighth graders into the NFL. Our idolatry of the rich convinces us that we need a "businessperson" to "straighten out" Washington. But running a business is not serving in political office, and our best presidents have been, not surprisingly, politicians. Followed by military leaders. Presidents whose primary pre–White House careers were in business (Harding, Coolidge, Trump) have been markedly less successful.

There are many reasons for this. One is that business teaches us to always look for the advantage, not to give anything away without getting more in return. That's the antithesis of government (and government service), whose purpose is to contribute to the commonwealth without recompense.

We should not rely on billionaires to save us. When your house is on fire and the wealthy guy from down the block shows up with a better hose to put out your fire, that doesn't mean we need more rich people on the block. It means we need to fund the fire department.

Philanthropy is less reliable and less accountable, and it doesn't scale well. Yet in the pandemic we look to Bill Gates to tell us what to do, as Dr. Fauci has been diminished. We wait for Tim Cook to get us masks, Elon Musk to supply ventilators, and Jeff Bezos to vaccinate us, because FEMA and the CDC aren't doing it. But predicating society on the unaccountable goodwill of billionaires is not a recipe for long-term prosperity. It's asking Pablo Escobar to fund the police.

## DEMOCRACY'S ONE WEIRD TRICK

How do we strengthen what we do control, our government?

What we've learned, through the Trump administration and especially during the pandemic, is that in a weak government, elected officials have more power than we realized, and institutions have less. Ironically, our national disregard for politicians has empowered them, because we've allowed them to hollow out the institutions meant to provide a long-term counterbalance. We've allowed *them* keep *us* in check.

People aren't very good at planning years ahead, en masse.

We want tax cuts, right now, over a cleaner environment for our children, decades from now. We surrender to our instincts for immediate gratification.[42]

Pure democracy is populism (*dêmos* is Ancient Greek for "ordinary citizens"). The *innovation* is institutions that slow democracy down and filter it through legislature, courts, and agencies. The media, too, is meant to have a countervailing effect—people with domain expertise who can say, "Let's interrogate the issue before banning immigrants from certain countries, removing grizzlies off endangered species lists, adding a citizenship question to the census, or restricting access to birth control because people in power at that moment decide it's a good idea."

## VOTE

The most important thing we can do is also the easiest. Vote. Vote in off-year elections. Vote in local elections. Because elected officials are defining government right now, and they respond to the demographics of the voting population. It matters much less who you vote for, than that you vote at all. The point is to signal that you are worth a politician's time. You want to know why we have a system that's designed to transfer wealth from the young to the old? Because old people vote. Those over 65 are twice as likely to vote as people under 30. And the *demo* in *democracy* works . . . too well. Politicians are even more likely to cater to even the old people who didn't vote for them. Because those are votes they can get. You know who politicians don't care about? Everyone who doesn't vote (or donate large amounts of money).

I think we should elect officials who believe in government, understand the threat of concentrated private power, and respect science. A broader electorate will mean that elected officials respond to the needs of a broader community.

## U.S. VOTER TURNOUT BY AGE

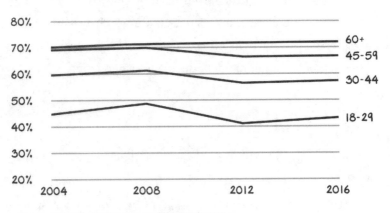

SOURCE: UNITED STATES ELECTION PROJECT.

## Tragedy of the Commons

Government is charged with preventing tragedies of the commons, so to speak. As I write this in August 2020, the immediate responsibility of government is to steer us through and out of the pandemic. I doubt that mission will have changed by the time this book goes to press. The history of missteps and chances lost in this pandemic is depressingly long, but the blame game is for historians, not serious leaders. We are facing an economic catastrophe, and we've already wasted the better part of $3 trillion not fixing it.

We need to protect people, not companies. My choice would have been to follow the German model. Under their "Kurzarbeit" program, employers can furlough workers during the pandemic, while the government takes responsibility for two thirds of the worker's salary. Workers stay technically employed, so they can easily return to their job once there is work to be done, but are under no pressure to work while it is unsafe. In effect, the government says, You don't need to worry about food. You are in a position where you can distance safely without putting your family at risk. You don't have to make bad decisions to feed your family. And there's no fear.[43] Happiness is not only a function of what you have, but what you don't have. Specifically, an absence of fear. Absence from the fear that you won't be able to feed your family or that serious illness might mean bankruptcy.

Other European countries have similar programs. In Spain, one worker told *The New York Times* that thanks to her country's aid, "I was able to feel relaxed at home." In Ireland, an event planner told the paper that since the government was paying his employees while they couldn't work, "It oddly hasn't been a stressful time." One of his employees was even able to complete the purchase of a house, remaining eligible for a mortgage because she was still technically employed.[44]

If that sounds expensive, consider America is still convulsed by the pandemic, while life has largely returned to normal in most of Europe and Asia. Or so we've heard. We can't see for ourselves, because EU countries will not let Americans in.

## DAILY NEW CONFIRMED COVID-19 CASES PER MILLION PEOPLE
### FEBRUARY 1 – AUGUST 7, 2020, ROLLING 7–DAY AVERAGE

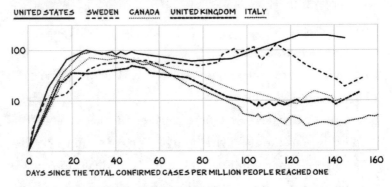

UNITED STATES    SWEDEN    CANADA    UNITED KINGDOM    ITALY

DAYS SINCE THE TOTAL CONFIRMED CASES PER MILLION PEOPLE REACHED ONE

SOURCE: OUR WORLD IN DATA. NOTE: LOG SCALE.

When you give money to poor and working-class people, you see an immediate multiplier effect in the economy—because they spend it. They buy food, they pay rent, they buy new shoes and fix their broken refrigerator. And consumers are the best arbiters of which companies should survive the crisis, not the government. If you believe in the power of markets, we should be putting money into the hands of consumers, not companies. The $1,200 checks the government sent out at the onset of the pandemic were a baby step in the right direction, but we are way past baby steps.

And I want to be clear: I'm not talking about unemployment insurance, though there is a role for that. We should take care of people who *can't* work, and aid during periods of unexpected job loss is an essential part of the safety net. But conditioning assistance on unemployment is needlessly disruptive on both employers and employees. For most people, it means losing health insurance. It requires complex administration, which as we have seen, breaks down in the face of high demand. The goal is to create jobs that endure in a post-pandemic economy.

The bulk of our economic response to the pandemic should have come in the form of protecting the people it puts at risk. Where it makes sense, by all means take action that ensures they will have jobs when it ends. But start with the people and work up. Don't start with shareholders and work down. Shareholders are supposed to lose, that's how capitalism works. The priorities are these: Protect people, not jobs. Protect jobs, not corporations. Protect corporations, not shareholders. End of list.


## CALLING THE CORONA CORPS

And we need to take the fight to the virus. Lockdowns are the nuclear option—social distancing and masking are necessary protections against an enemy on the march. Epidemics either burn themselves out (and this one would likely kill millions if we let it do that) or are defeated through aggressive containment measures. South Korea has even published a playbook.[45]

The proven formula for flattening the curve without putting the economy back in an induced coma is simple: testing, tracing, and isolation. That is, we need widespread testing followed by the swift identification and temporary isolation of everyone who has come in contact with infected people. In a country as large as ours, with the virus as widespread as it is, it would take an army to do that now. Estimates range, but we need something close to 180,000 contact tracers. Fortunately, we have an army waiting in the wings.

Recent high school graduates face an unpalatable choice: the worst job market in modern history, or a $50,000 streaming video platform called College in the Time of Corona. We should put them to work in a Corona Corps, an organization in the long tradition of youth service, from Mormon missionaries to Teach for America to the Peace Corps, but one focused on the crisis at hand. A volunteer army of 18- to 24-year-olds, trained and equipped to fight the virus—and reshape the trajectory of their own lives.

The Corps' main job would be contact tracing: interviewing infected people, evaluating the nature of their contacts and reaching out to those put at risk. The Corps would also staff testing centers across the country and work with people who are required to isolate, providing anything from food delivery to emotional support. The government-funded Corona Corps would pay their costs and a modest wage, say $2,500 a month. Those who serve at least six months would receive a credit toward educational costs or student debt.

Beyond the benefits that would accrue to those who serve, and the role they would play in defeating the virus, I believe the country would reap a larger dividend. A service program like this could help bridge partisan divides. Consider that between 1965 and 1975, more than two thirds of the members of Congress had served their country in uniform. The important legislative achievements of those years were shaped by leaders who shared that bond, larger than politics or party. Today, fewer than 20 percent have that bond. The Corps, and future national service programs, could reanimate our superpower, cooperation.

Service in the Corps would not be without risk. But we send young people to the front lines of wars not because they are immune from bullets, but because someone must go. And young adults appear to face much lower risk of serious side effects or death from Covid-19 than older people. Corps members would be regularly tested, and if they were infected, they have an overwhelming likelihood not just of recovering, but of developing antibodies.

A Corona Corps would not be cheap: 180,000 members at, I estimate, $60,000 each for compensation, training, and support would cost nearly $11 billion. The government could no doubt find a way to make it cost twice that. Yet that's a rounding error on the sums allocated for stimulus and unemployment to date. Consider it a warranty against needing another multitrillion-dollar rescue package.

Moreover, the Corona Corps could be the nucleus of a permanent national service organization. An opportunity to mature a generation of Americans who might sit or stand shoulder to shoulder and see each other, first and foremost, as Americans instead of Democrats or Republicans. We need our young people grounded, again, in America.

## MALEFACTORS OF GREAT WEALTH

Addressing the current crisis is just the beginning of government responsibilities, of course. Looking ahead, there are two priorities that should inform our policies: restraining private power, especially that held by big tech, and empowering individuals.

The first step to restraining private power is to get it out of government. Ideally we would substantially reduce the amount of money that flows from private wealth into political campaigns, though the Supreme Court has made that difficult. The least we can do, however, is enforce the bright-line rules against outright corruption. We've got to take conflict-of-interest rules seriously. When elected to national office, your assets should go in a blind trust. Permitting politicians to trade stock on information they obtain undermines faith in our institutions. A study of stock trades by senators in the 1990s found they beat the market by about 12% per year—twice the advantage enjoyed by corporate insiders.[46] In May 2020, Senator Richard Burr had access to confidential information about the seriousness of the coronavirus, and then appears to have used that to time his stock trades. Future senators shouldn't be tempted to engage in this type of corruption. Likewise, it's lunacy that we don't require presidential candidates to release their tax returns, or enforce the constitutional prohibition on presidents profiting from their office.

Beyond cleaning its own house, Congress and the Executive must reinvigorate our antitrust and regulatory limits, particularly on big tech. I've touched on this in chapter 2, so here I only want to emphasize the power of these remedies. Regulation can be freeing. I don't think the managers at the GM plant *want* to pour mercury in the river. But why disarm unilaterally? Business is hard enough without making it a daily morality test. Environmental laws make it easier to do the right thing.

Likewise, we think of antitrust (breaking companies up) as a punishment. It isn't, it's oxygenation. When we broke up AT&T we birthed seven firms that in aggregate were worth more than the original. According to one analysis, an investment in AT&T on the eve of the breakup in 1983 returned an annual growth rate of 18.5% through 1995, while the broader market grew at around 10% over the same period. One of the divested companies, Southwestern Bell, was so successful that it bought AT&T itself in 2005. As for the rest of us not fortunate enough to have AT&T stock in 1983, compare the innovation during the twenty years pre breakup (touch-tone dialing and call waiting) to post breakup (cell phones, the consumer internet, and the then-longest bull market in history).

If you set aside the notion of antitrust enforcement as a moral judgment and consider the advantages, many of the problems posed by big tech—not all of them—would be addressed if these companies were broken up. If we split Google and YouTube into separate companies, we wouldn't create competition directly. But at the first board meeting of the newly spun YouTube, new leadership would decide to get into text-based search. Across town at the first board meeting of the new Google, the firm likely decides to get into video-based search.

Competition creates options. As a monopoly, why would YouTube improve its kids' content when there is no competing video platform with more effective guardrails? Someone at one of these board meetings will realize Procter & Gamble is more likely to advertise on their video platform if they commit to protecting young viewers. And that Unilever is more inclined to patronize a search engine that ensures when someone types in "overthrow the government," the first result is a voter regis- tration form and not instructions on how to build a dirty bomb.

Currently, there's no incentive to do anything but create algorithms that inspire more clicks and more addiction, not giving a damn about the commonwealth. So, we break them up—not because they're evil, not because they don't pay their taxes, not because they destroy jobs—but because we're capi- talists, and we believe in competition and innovation. It's not punishment, it's overdue oxygenation of the marketplace that will unleash billions, maybe trillions, in shareholder value.

## What We Must Do

I opened this book with some statistics about wars: World War II, a war of sacrifice, and the war against Covid, a battle of selfish behavior vs. a pathogen. And it appears we are losing this battle, and maybe the larger war. This microscopic foe has exploited flaws in our society. It kills a thousand of us each day—many times the death rate of past wars. We have mobilized, in a sense, but not well.

Once, we fought on multiple fronts—home and abroad, technological, industrial, and agricultural, political and personal. In WWII almost a third of vegetables were harvested from "victory gardens" planted in people's yards. Eleanor Roosevelt planted one on the White House lawn.

Despite the formidable financial stress of wartime, house-

holds were asked to dig deeper and buy war bonds. The entire auto industry was retooled to build bombers and tanks—not a single new car was built for almost three years.[47] Chrysler built a factory in the Detroit suburbs that manufactured more tanks than the entire Third Reich.[48] And a generation of young men heeded the call to arms, 450,000 dying on the beaches of Normandy and the jungles of Luzon. Sure, we had plans for a silver bullet: 120,000 people worked on the Manhattan Project to find a vaccine for tyranny. But we didn't stop planting victory gardens, building tanks, and sacrificing while we waited for Einstein and Oppenheimer to save us.

Not all of this was popular, and none of it was easy. Angry and desperate people counterfeited ration cards, evaded travel restrictions, and over 5,000 Americans were imprisoned for evading the draft.[49] The government invested millions in enforcement— but also encouragement. From the White House to Hollywood, public figures called on patriotism and crafted a shared purpose to inspire widespread sacrifice.

Our patriotic sacrifices in WWII were not inevitable. We were called to them by leaders who knew what was required of us, and laid it out for us in honest terms. At every level, and in every field, voices were raised in support of the commonwealth, rather than in defense of personal property and a perverted sense of freedom.

Where is that shared purpose today? We are fighting an enemy three times as lethal to our population as the Axis powers, yet Americans don't want to wear masks and expect the government to send them more money. Resistance to sacrifice and dismissal of community is framed as "liberty."

Liberty is a founding American value, but it is not an individual guarantee, nor one divorced from the greater good. This is the central thesis of the Declaration of Independence: not merely that life, liberty, and the pursuit of happiness are inalienable rights, but that "to secure these rights, Governments are instituted among Men." The Founders, as imperfect as they were, saw clearly what we have forgotten. As Benjamin Franklin said when he signed the revolutionary document, "We must all hang together, or, most assuredly, we shall hang separately."

We didn't need to be here, and we are not doomed to continue down this path. Indeed, the good news is that defeating the pandemic and moving from crisis to opportunity requires that we reawaken our national character. The opportunity presented by such a reawakening is immense.

> *A step backward, after making a wrong turn, is a step in the right direction.*
>
> —KURT VONNEGUT

Pandemics, wars, depressions—these shocks are painful, but the times that follow are often among the most productive in human history. The generations that endure and observe the pain are best prepared for the fight.

How will the rising generation shoulder the burdens of the post-corona world? There is reason to hope.

Might we be maturing a generation that will embrace our species' superpower: cooperation? If the British, Russians, and Americans could partner to fight a common enemy 80 years ago, can't we partner to eradicate an enemy that threatens all 7.7 billion of us?

Might this generation decide that if half our nation's population cannot go 60 days without government assistance, then we must make more forward-leaning investments to save trillions in future emergency stimulus?

Might this generation inspire greater comity of man, more empathy for the disenfranchised, and a greater appreciation for what it means to be American? And finally, might we decide to reinvest in the greatest source of good in history—the U.S. government? Might we?

America's history is not short on crises or missed opportunities. Its sins and failures are as historic as its virtues and successes. At its best, America exemplifies generosity, grit, innovation, and a willingness to sacrifice for one another and for future generations. When we lose sight of these, we wander into exploitation and crisis.

All of our history, as well as our future, is *ours*. Our commonwealth didn't just happen, it was shaped. We chose this path—no trend is permanent and can't be made worse or corrected.

America isn't "what it is," but what we make of it.

# ACKNOWLEDGMENTS

Greatness is in the agency of others, as was this book.

Every time I finish a book, I swear that it will be the last one. Then my agent, Jim Levine, convinces me to write another. He is an inspiration, and the inspiration for this book.

Jason Stavers and Maria Petrova did the heavy lifting, taking my drafts, my notes, my late-night emails, and shaping them into a narrative. Jason has been working with me for twenty-five years, and can finish my sentences . . . as he did repeatedly here. Maria edits in her fourth language, and her skill dwarfs our facility with our first.

My data and creative teams inspire my ideas and make them pop—I wouldn't be half as informative or entertaining without them. Taylor Malmsheimer, Mia Silverio, Griffin Carlborg, and James Steiner find the diamonds in the rough world of data.

Jerllin Cheng, Radhika Patel, Ted Munro, and Christopher Gonzalez polish, visualize, and make them memorable. Katherine Dillon orchestrates it all and, with Aaron Bunge, developed the cover.

Finally, Adrian Zackheim and Niki Papadopoulos, and their entire team at Portfolio, keep the work honest and on track.

I am grateful for everyone's good work and generosity.

# NOTES

## INTRODUCTION

1. Falcon, Andrea. "Time for Aristotle," *Notre Dame Philosophical Reviews*, April 1, 2006. https://ndpr.nd.edu/news/time-for-aristotle/.
2. Parker, Kim, Juliana Menasce Horowitz, and Anna Brown, "About Half of Lower-Income Americans Report Household Job or Wage Loss Due to COVID-19." Pew Research Center, April 21, 2020. https://www.pew socialtrends.org/2020/04/21/about-half-of-lower-income-americans -report-household-job-or-wage-loss-due-to-covid-19/.
3. Iacurci, Greg. "40% of Low-Income Americans Lost Their Jobs Due to the Pandemic," CNBC, May 14, 2020. https://www.cnbc.com/2020/05 /14/40percent-of-low-income-americans-lost-their-jobs-in-march -according-to-fed.html.
4. Davis, Dominic-Madori. "Over 2 Million Gen Zers Have Moved Back In with Family in the Wake of the Coronavirus," *Business Insider*, August 1, 2020. https://www.businessinsider.com/gen-zers-moved-back-with-par ents-family-coronavirus-zillow-studoc-2020-7.
5. An account of rationing imposed during WWII and its effects on domestic life: Flamm, Bradley J. "Putting the Brakes on 'Non-Essential' Travel: 1940s Wartime Mobility, Prosperity, and the US Office of Defense." *Journal of Transport History* 27, no. 1 (2006): 71–92. https://www.researchgate .net/publication/233547720_Putting_the_brakes_on_%27non-essential

%27_travel_1940s_wartime_mobility_prosperity_and_the_US_Office_of
_Defense. See also this compelling essay about how the U.S. united in
the war effort, including setting the speed limit to 35 miles per hour so as
to preserve tires: Davis, Wade. "The Unraveling of America," *Rolling
Stone*, August 6, 2020. https://www.rollingstone.com/politics/political
-commentary/covid-19-end-of-american-era-wade-davis-1038206/.

6. Macias, Amanda. "America Has Spent $6.4 Trillion on Wars in the Mid-
   dle East and Asia Since 2001, a New Study Says," CNBC, November 20,
   2019.   https://www.cnbc.com/2019/11/20/us-spent-6point4-trillion-on
   -middle-east-wars-since-2001-study.html.

7. Koma, Wyatt et al. "Low-Income and Communities of Color at Higher
   Risk of Serious Illness if Infected with Coronavirus," KFF, May 7, 2020.
   https://www.kff.org/coronavirus-covid-19/issue-brief/low-income-and
   -communities-of-color-at-higher-risk-of-serious-illness-if-infected-with
   -coronavirus/.

## CHAPTER ONE: COVID & THE CULLING

1. Lee, Justina and Valdana Hajric. "Why Robinhood Day Traders Are
   Greedy When Wall Street Is Fearful," *Bloomberg Businessweek*, June 11,
   2020.  https://www.bloomberg.com/news/articles/2020-06-11/u-s-stock
   -market-investors-keep-buying-amid-recession.

2. Cain, Áine and Madeline Stone. "These 31 Retailers and Restaurant Companies Have Filed for Bankruptcy or Liquidation in 2020," *Business Insider*, August 25, 2020. https://www.businessinsider.com/retailers-filed
   -bankruptcy-liquidation-closing-stores-2020-2#california-pizza-kitchen
   -filed-for-chapter-11-bankruptcy-on-july-30-after-permanently
   -closing-an-undisclosed-number-of-restaurants-due-to-the-pandemic-26.

3. Neufeld, Dorothy. "The Hardest Hit Companies of the COVID-19 Downturn: The 'BEACH' Stocks," Visual Capitalist, March 25, 2020. https://
   www.visualcapitalist.com/covid-19-downturn-beach-stocks/.

4. Swisher, Kara and Scott Galloway, hosts. "Addressing the US economy (a
   note from Andrew Yang), data privacy in a public health emergency, and
   a listener question on the 'great WFH-experiment,'" *Pivot* (podcast),
   March 20, 2020.

5. "James Provisions: Brooklyn." jamesrestaurantny.com.

6. Olsen, Parmy. "Telemedicine, Once a Hard Sell, Can't Keep Up with
   Demand," *Wall Street Journal*, April 1, 2020. https://www.wsj.com/arti
   cles/telemedicine-once-a-hard-sell-cant-keep-up-with-demand
   -11585734425.

7. Forman, Laura. "The Pandemic Has Made Sudden Heroes of the Tech Companies—for Now," *Wall Street Journal*, May 8, 2020. https://www.wsj.com/articles/the-pandemic-has-made-sudden-heroes-of-the-tech-companiesfor-now-11588930200.

8. Davis, Michelle F. and Jeff Green. "Three Hours Longer, the Pandemic Workday Has Obliterated Work-Life Balance: People Are Overworked, Stressed, and Eager to Get Back to the Office," *Bloomberg*, April 23, 2020. https://www.bloomberg.com/news/articles/2020-04-23/working-from-home-in-covid-era-means-three-more-hours-on-the-job?sref=AhQQoPzF.

9. Mims, Christopher. "The Work-from-Home Shift Shocked Companies—Now They're Learning Its Lessons," *Wall Street Journal*, July 25, 2020. https://www.wsj.com/articles/the-work-from-home-shift-shocked-companiesnow-theyre-learning-its-lessons-11595649628.

10. Mims, "The Work-from-Home Shift."

11. Ingraham, Christopher. "Nine Days on the Road. Average Commute Time Reached a New Record Last Year," *Washington Post*, October 7, 2019. https://www.washingtonpost.com/business/2019/10/07/nine-days-road-average-commute-time-reached-new-record-Last-year/.

12. Galloway, Scott. "WeWTF," *No Mercy / No Malice* (blog), August 16, 2019. https://profgalloway.com/wewtf. See also Walsh, James D. "'At What Point Does Malfeasance Become Fraud?': NYU Biz-School Professor Scott Galloway on WeWork," *New York Magazine*, October 1, 2019. https://nymag.com/intelligencer/2019/10/marketing-expert-scott-galloway-on-wework-and-adam-neumann.html.

13. "Coca Cola Commercial—I'd Like to Teach the World to Sing (In Perfect Harmony)—1971." Uploaded December 29, 2008. Video, 00:59. https://youtu.be/ib-Qiyklq-Q.

14. Perrin, Nicole. "Facebook-Google Duopoly Won't Crack This Year," eMarketer, November 4, 2019. https://www.emarketer.com/content/facebook-google-duopoly-won-t-crack-this-year.

15. Gill, Zinnia. "Magna Forecasts V-Shaped Recovery for the US Advertising Market," MAGNA, March 26, 2020. https://magnaglobal.com/magna-forecasts-v-shaped-recovery-for-the-us-advertising-market/.

16. McArdie, Megan. "Don't Just Look at Covid-19 Fatality Rates, Look at People Who Survive But Don't Entirely Recover," *Washington Post*, August 16, 2020. https://www.washingtonpost.com/opinions/dont-just-look-at-covid-19-fatality-rates-look-at-people-who-survive--but-dont-entirely-recover/2020/08/14/3b3de170-de6a-11ea-8051-d5f887d73381_story.html.

17. Chuck, Elizabeth and Chelsea Bailey. "Apple CEO Tim Cook Slams Facebook: Privacy 'Is a Human Right, It's a Civil Liberty.'" NBC News, March

28, 2018. https://www.nbcnews.com/tech/tech-news/apple-ceo-tim-cook -slams-facebook-privacy-human-right-it-n860816.

18. Smith, Chris. "Making the $1,249 iPhone Xs Only Costs Apple $443," *New York Post*, September 26, 2018. https://nypost.com/2018/09/26 /making-the-1249-iphone-xs-only-costs-apple-443/.

19. Lyons, Kim. "TikTok Says It Will Stop Accessing Clipboard Content on iOS Devices: A Beta Feature on iOS 14 Showed What the App Was Up To," The Verge, June 26, 2020. https://www.theverge.com/2020/6/26 /21304228/tiktok-security-ios-clipboard-access-ios14-beta-feature.

20. Galloway, Scott. "Four Weddings & a Funeral," *No Mercy / No Malice* (blog), June 12 2020. https://www.profgalloway.com/four-weddings-a-funeral.

21. Rodriguez, Salvador. "Why Facebook Generates Much More Money Per User Than Its Rivals," CNBC, November 1, 2019. https://www.cnbc .com/2019/11/01/facebook-towers-over-rivals-in-the-critical-metric-of -revenue-per-user.html.

22. Tran, Kevin. "LinkedIn Looks to Become Dominant Ad Force," *Business Insider*, September 7, 2017. https://www.businessinsider.com/linkedin -looks-to-become-dominant-ad-force-2017-9.

## CHAPTER TWO: THE FOUR

1. Li, Yun. "The Five Biggest Stocks Are Dwarfing the Rest of the Stock Market at an 'Unprecedented' Level." CNBC, January 13, 2020. https:// www.cnbc.com/2020/01/13/five-biggest-stocks-dwarfing-the -market-at-unprecedented-level.html.

2. Bowman, Jeremy. "Jet.com May Be History, but Walmart Got What It Needed," Motley Fool, May 20, 2020. https://www.fool.com/investing /2020/05/20/jetcom-may-be-history-but-walmart-got-what-it-need .aspx; https://www.axios.com/walmart-jet-com-6502ec3f-090c-4761 -9620-944f99603719.html.

3. Dunne, Chris. "15 Amazon Statistics You Need to Know in 2020," Repri-cerexpress, last visited September 3, 2020. https://www.repricerex press.com/amazon-statistics/.

4. O'Hara, Andrew. "Apple's Wearables Division Now Size of Fortune 140 Company," Apple Insider, last accessed September 3, 2020. https:// appleinsider.com/articles/20/04/30/apples-wearables-division-now -size-of-fortune-140-company.

5. Galloway, Scott. "Stream On," *No Mercy / No Malice* (blog), November 22, 2019. https://www.profgalloway.com/stream-on.

6. Brush, Michael. "Opinion: Here's Why Netflix Stock, Now Below $500, Is Going to $1,000," MarketWatch, August 1, 2020. https://www.mar ketwatch.com/story/heres-why-netflix-stock-now-below-500-is-going -to-1000-2020-07-27/.

7. Knibbs, Kate. "Laughing at Quibi Is Way More Fun Than Watching Quibi," *Wired*, July 15, 2020. https://www.wired.com/story/quibi -schadenfreude/.

8. Goldberg, Lesley. "Inside Apple's Long, Bumpy Road to Hollywood." *Hollywood Reporter*, October 15, 2019. https://www.hollywoodreporter .com/news/apples-bumpy-tv-launch-inside-tech-giants-impending -arrival-hollywood-1247577.

9. Milan, Aiden. "How Much Did Each *Game of Thrones* Season Cost to Make?" *Metro*, May 21, 2019. https://metro.co.uk/2019/05/21/much -game-thrones-season-cost-make-9622963/.

10. Solsman, Joan E. "HBO Max: Everything to Know About HBO's Bigger Streaming App," CNET, August 28, 2020. https://www.cnet.com/news /hbo-max-live-everything-to-know-go-roku-amazon-firestick -streaming-app/.

11. Gomes, Lee. "Microsoft Will Pay $275 Million to Settle Lawsuit from Caldera," *Wall Street Journal*, January 11, 2000. https://www.wsj.com /articles/SB947543007415899052.

12. Mac, Ryan. "A Kenosha Militia Facebook Event Asking Attendees to Bring Weapons Was Reported 455 Times. Moderators Said It Didn't Violate Any Rules," *BuzzFeed News*, August 28, 2020. https://www .buzzfeednews.com/article/ryanmac/kenosha-militia-facebook -reported-455-times-moderators.

13. Wong, Julia Carrie. "Praise for Alleged Kenosha Shooter Proliferates on Facebook Despite Supposed Ban," *Guardian*, August 27, 2020. https:// www.theguardian.com/technology/2020/aug/27/facebook-kenosha -shooter-support-ban.

14. Townsend, Mark. "Facebook Algorithm Found to 'Actively Promote' Ho-locaust Denial," *Guardian*, August 16, 2020. https://www.theguardian .com/world/2020/aug/16/facebook-algorithm-found-to-actively -promote-holocaust-denial.

15. Collins, Ben and Brandy Zadronzy. "QAnon Groups Hit by Face-book Crackdown," NBC News, August 19, 2020. https://www.nbcnews .com/tech/tech-news/qanon-groups-hit-facebook-crack-down -n1237330.

16. Galloway, Scott and Aswath Damodaran. "Valuing Tech's Titans," *Win-ners & Losers*, July 27, 2017. Video series, 37:27. https://www.youtube .com/watch?v=4CLEuPfwVBo.

17. Weise, Karen. "Amazon Sells More, but Warns of Much Higher Costs Ahead," *New York Times*, April 30, 2020. https://www.nytimes.com /2020/04/30/technology/amazon-stock-earnings-report.html.

18. Bohn, Dieter. "Amazon Announces Halo, a Fitness Band and App That Scans Your Body and Voice," The Verge, August 27, 2020. https://www .theverge.com/2020/8/27/21402493/amazon-halo-band-health-fitness -body-scan-tone-emotion-activity-sleep.

19. Murphy, Mike. "There Are Signs of Life for Apple Beyond the iPhone," Quartz, October 30, 2019. https://qz.com/1738780/apples-q4-2019 -earnings-show-the-iphone-isnt-all-that-matters/.

20. Leswing, Kif. "Apple Is Laying the Groundwork for an iPhone Sub- scription," CNBC, October 30, 2019. https://www.cnbc.com/2019/10/30 /apple-lays-groundwork-for-iphone-or-apple-prime-subscription .html.

21. "Sources of Funds," California State University, 2019–20 Operating Bud- get, last accessed September 3, 2020. https://www2.calstate.edu/csu -system/about-the-csu/budget/2019-20-operating-budget/2019-20 -operating-budget-plan.

22. Hsu, Tiffany and Eleanor Lutz. "More Than 1,000 Companies Boycotted Facebook. Did It Work?" *New York Times*, August 1, 2020. https://www .nytimes.com/2020/08/01/business/media/facebook-boycott.html?ac tion=click&module=Well&pgtype=Homepage&section=Business.

23. Stoller, Matt. "Absentee Ownership: How Amazon, Facebook, and Google Ruin Commerce Without Noticing," "BIG," July 28, 2020. https://matt stoller.substack.com/p/absentee-ownership-how-amazon-facebook.

## CHAPTER THREE: OTHER DISRUPTORS

1. U.S. Bureau of Labor Statistics. https://www.bls.gov/.

2. Adamczyk, Alicia. "Health Insurance Premiums Increased More Than Wages This Year," CNBC, September 26, 2019. https://www.cnbc.com /2019/09/26/health-insurance-premiums-increased-more-than-wages -this-year.html.

3. Lee, Aileen. "Welcome to the Unicorn Club: Learning from Billion- Dollar Startups," TechCrunch, November 2, 2013. https://techcrunch .com/2013/11/02/welcome-to-the-unicorn-club/.

4. Teare, Gené. "Private Unicorn Board Now Above 600 Companies Valued at $2T," Crunchbase, June 29, 2020. https://news.crunchbase .com/news/private-unicorn-board-now-above-600-companies -valued-at-2t/.

5. Smith, Gerry and Mark Gurman. "Apple Plans Mega Bundle of Music, News, TV as Early as 2020," *Bloomberg*, November 14, 2019. https://www.bloomberg.com/news/articles/2019-11-14/apple-mulls-bundling-digital-subscriptions-as-soon-as-2020?sref=AhQQoPzF.

6. Roof, Katie and Olivia Carville. "Airbnb Quarterly Revenue Drops 67%; IPO Still Planned," *Bloomberg*, August 12, 2020. https://www.bloomberg.com/news/articles/2020-08-12/airbnb-revenue-tanks-67-in-second-quarter-ipo-planned-for-2020?sref=AhQQoPzF.

7. Witkowski, Wallace. "Lemonade IPO: 5 Things to Know About the Online Insurer," MarketWatch, July 2, 2020. https://www.marketwatch.com/story/lemonade-ipo-5-things-to-know-about-the-online-insurer-2020-07-01.

8. "Investor Relations," Peloton, last accessed September 3, 2020. https://investor.onepeloton.com/investor-relations.

9. Watson, Amy. "Video Content Budget of Netflix Worldwide from 2013 to 2020," Statista, May 28, 2020. https://www.statista.com/statistics/707302/netflix-video-content-budget/.

10. *Tiger King* (TV series). Directed by Eric Goode and Rebecca Chaiklin, 2020. Netflix.

11. "Tesla's Recent Rally Comes from Its Narrative, Not the News or Fundamentals, Says NYU's Aswath Damodaran." Video. CNBC, July 9, 2020. https://www.cnbc.com/video/2020/07/09/teslas-recent-rally-comes-from-its-narrative-not-the-news-or-fundamentals-says-nyus-aswath-damodaran.html.

12. Isaac, Mike. *Super Pumped: The Battle for Uber* (New York: W. W. Norton & Company, 2019). An interesting and cinematic account of Kalanick's years at Uber and the transition to Khosrowshahi.

13. Chen, Brian X. and Taylor Lorenz. "We Tested Instagram Reels, the TikTok Clone. What a Dud," *New York Times*, August 14, 2020. https://www.nytimes.com/2020/08/12/technology/personaltech/tested-facebook-reels-tiktok-clone-dud.html.

14. KPMG International. "Venture Capital Remains Resilient," PR Newswire, July 22, 2020. https://www.prnewswire.com/news-releases/venture-capital-remains-resilient,Äîus62-9-billion-raised-by-vc-backed-companies-in-the-second-quarter-according-to-kpmg-private-enterprises-global-venture-pulse-q220-report-301097576.html.

## CHAPTER FOUR: HIGHER EDUCATION

1. Kamal, Rabah, Daniel McDermott, and Cynthia Cox. "How Has US Spending on Healthcare Changed over Time?" Health System Tracker,

December 20, 2019. https://www.healthsystemtracker.org/chart-collec tion/u-s-spending-healthcare-changed-time/#item-nhe-trends_total -national-health-expenditures-us-per-capita-1970-2018.

2. Galloway, Scott. "Getting the Easy Stuff Right," *No Mercy / No Malice* (blog), December 14, 2018. https://www.profgalloway.com/getting-the -easy-stuff-right.

3. Galloway, Scott. "Gang of Four: Apple / Amazon / Facebook / Google (Scott Galloway, Founder of L2) | DLD16." Talk at DLD Conference, Munich, Germany, January 25, 2016. Video, 16:18. https://www.youtube .com/watch?v=jfjg0kGQFBY.

4. Walsh, Brian. "The Dirty Secret of Elite College Admissions," Medium, December 12, 2018. https://gen.medium.com/the-dirty-secret-of-elite -college-admissions-d41077df670e.

5. Gage, John. "Harvard Newspaper Survey Finds 1% of Faculty Members Identify as Conservative," *Washington Examiner*, March 4, 2020. https:// www.washingtonexaminer.com/news/harvard-newspaper-survey -finds-1-of-faculty-members-identify-as-conservative.

6. Carey, Kevin. "The 'Public' in Public College Could Be Endangered," *New York Times*, May 5, 2020. https://www.nytimes.com/2020/05/05 /upshot/public-colleges-endangered-pandemic.html.

7. Miller, Ben et al. "Addressing the $1.5 Trillion in Federal Student Loan Debt." Center for American Progress, June 12, 2019. https://www.amer icanprogress.org/issues/education-postsecondary/reports/2019/06/12 /470893/addressing-1-5-trillion-federal-student-loan-debt/.

8. Fain, Paul. "Wealth's Influence on Enrollment and Completion," Inside Higher Ed, May 23, 2019. https://www.insidehighered.com/news/2019 /05/23/feds-release-broader-data-socioeconomic-status-and-college -enrollment-and-completion.

9. Aisch, Gregor et al. "Some Colleges Have More Students from the Top 1 Percent Than the Bottom 60. Find Yours," *New York Times*, January 18, 2017. https://www.nytimes.com/interactive/2017/01/18/upshot/some -colleges-have-more-students-from-the-top-1-percent-than-the -bottom-60.html.

10. Leighton, Mara. "Yale's Most Popular Class Ever Is Available Free Online—and the Topic Is How to Be Happier in Your Daily Life," *Business Insider*, July 13, 2020. https://www.businessinsider.com/coursera -yale-science-of-wellbeing-free-course-review-overview.

11. Selingo, Jeffrey J. "Despite Strong Economy, Worrying Financial Signs for Higher Education," *Washington Post*, August 3, 2018. https://www .washingtonpost.com/news/grade-point/wp/2018/08/03/despite -strong-economy-worrying-financial-signs-for-higher-education/.

12. Christensen, Clayton M. and Michael B. Horn. "Innovation Imperative: Change Everything," *New York Times*, November 1, 2013. https://www.nytimes.com/2013/11/03/education/edlife/online-education-as-an-agent-of-transformation.html.

13. Hess, Abigail. "Harvard Business School Professor: Half of American Colleges Will Be Bankrupt in 10 to 15 Years," CNBC, August 30, 2018. https://www.cnbc.com/2018/08/30/hbs-prof-says-half-of-us-colleges-will-be-bankrupt-in-10-to-15-years.html.

14. Oneclass Blog. "75% of College Students Unhappy with Quality of eLearning During Covid-19," *OneClass* (blog), April 1, 2020. https://oneclass.com/blog/featured/177356-7525-of-college-students-unhappy-with-quality-of-elearning-during-covid-19.en.html.

15. "Looking Ahead to Fall 2020: How Covid-19 Continues to Influence the Choice of College-Going Students." Art and Science Group LLC, April 2020. https://www.artsci.com/studentpoll-covid-19-edition-2.

16. "The College Crisis Initiative." @Davidson College, last accessed September 3, 2020. https://collegecrisis.shinyapps.io/dashboard/.

17. Lapp, Katie. "Update on Operational and Financial Planning," Harvard University, June 9, 2020. https://www.harvard.edu/update-on-operational-and-financial-planning.

18. Carey, Kevin. "Risky Strategy by Many Private Colleges Leaves Them Exposed," *New York Times*, May 26, 2020. https://www.nytimes.com/2020/05/26/upshot/virus-colleges-risky-strategy.html.

19. Steinberg, Laurence. "Expecting Students to Play It Safe if Colleges Reopen Is a Fantasy," *New York Times*, June 15, 2020. https://www.nytimes.com/2020/06/15/opinion/coronavirus-college-safe.html.

20. Field, Anne. "10 Great Places to Live and Learn," AARP.org. https://www.aarp.org/retirement/planning-for-retirement/info-2016/ten-ideal-college-towns-for-retirement-photo.html.

21. Zong, Jie and Jeanne Batalova. "International Students in the United States." Migration Policy Institute, May 9, 2018. https://www.migrationpolicy.org/article/international-students-united-states-2017.

22. Whiteman, Doug. "These Chains Are Permanently Closing the Most Stores in 2020," MoneyWise, August 12, 2020. https://moneywise.com/a/chains-closing-the-most-stores-in-2020.

23. Thomas, Lauren. "25,000 Stores Are Predicted to Close in 2020, as the Coronavirus Pandemic Accelerates Industry Upheaval," CNBC, June 9, 2020. https://www.cnbc.com/2020/06/09/coresight-predicts-record-25000-retail-stores-will-close-in-2020.html.

24. "Public Viewpoint: COVID-19 Work and Education Survey," STRADA: Center for Consumer Insights, July 29, 2020. https://www.strada

education.org/wp-content/uploads/2020/07/Report-July-29-2020
.pdf.

25. Galloway, Scott. "Cash & Denting the Universe," *No Mercy / No Malice*
(blog), May 5, 2017. https://www.profgalloway.com/cash-denting-the
-universe.

26. Bariso, Justin. "Google's Plan to Disrupt the College Degree Is Absolute
Genius." *Inc.*, August 24, 2020. https://www.inc.com/justin-bariso
/google-career-certificates-plan-disrupt-college-degree-university
-genius.html.

27. Bridgeland, John M. and John J. DiIulio Jr. "Will America Embrace National Service?" Brookings Institution, October 2019. https://www.brook
ings.edu/wp-content/uploads/2019/10/National-Service_TEXT-3.pdf.

28. Spees, Ann-Cathrin. "Could Germany's Vocational Education and
Training System Be a Model for the U.S.?" *World Education News + Reviews*, June 12, 2018. https://wenr.wes.org/2018/06/could-germanys
-vocational-education-and-training-system-be-a-model-for-the-u-s; and
a great book on the subject by Matthew Crawford, *Shop Class as Soul-
craft: An Inquiry into the Value of Work* (New York: Penguin Books, 2009).

## CHAPTER FIVE: THE COMMONWEALTH

1. Harari, Yuval Noah. *Sapiens: A Brief History of Humankind* (New York:
Harper Perennial, 2018), 25.

2. McIntosh, Kristen et al. "Examining the Black-White Wealth Gap."
Brookings Institution, February 27, 2020. https://www.brookings.edu
/blog/up-front/2020/02/27/examining-the-black-white-wealth-gap/.

3. Aisch, Gregor et al. "Some Colleges Have More Students From the Top 1
Percent Than the Bottom 60. Find Yours," *New York Times*, January 18,
2017. https://www.nytimes.com/interactive/2017/01/18/upshot/some
-colleges-have-more-students-from-the-top-1-percent-than-the
-bottom-60.html.

4. Maciag, Mike. "Your ZIP Code Determines Your Life Expectancy, But
Not in These 7 Places," Governing.com, November 2018. https://www
.governing.com/topics/health-human-services/gov-neighborhood-life
-expectancy.html; https://time.com/5608268/zip-code-health/.

5. Kahneman, Daniel. *Thinking, Fast and Slow* (New York: Farrar, Straus
and Giroux, 2011).

6. "About Chronic Diseases." Centers for Disease Control and Prevention,
last accessed September 3, 2020. https://www.cdc.gov/chronicdisease
/about/costs/index.htm.

7. "CDC—Budget Request Overview." Centers for Disease Control and Prevention. https://www.cdc.gov/budget/documents/fy2020/cdc-overview -factsheet.pdf.

8. Stein, Jeff. "Tax Change in Coronavirus Package Overwhelmingly Benefits Millionaires, Congressional Body Finds," *Washington Post*, April 14, 2020. https://www.washingtonpost.com/business/2020/04 /14/coronavirus-law-congress-tax-change/.

9. Woods, Hiat. "How Billionaires Got $637 Billion Richer During the Coronavirus Pandemic," *Business Insider*, August 3, 2020. https://www .businessinsider.com/billionaires-net-worth-increases-coronavirus -pandemic-2020-7. See also Mims, Christopher. "Covid-19 Is Dividing the American Worker," *Wall Street Journal*, August 22, 2020. https:// www.wsj.com/articles/covid-19-is-dividing-the-american-worker -11598068859. The author says we have a "'K' shaped recovery . . . in which there are now two Americas: professionals who are largely back to work, with stock portfolios approaching new highs, and everyone else."

10. Kiel, Paul and Justin Elliott. "Trump Administration Discloses Some Recipients of $670 Billion Small Business Bailout," ProPublica, July 6, 2020. https://www.propublica.org/article/trump-administration-discloses -some-recipients-of-670-billion-small-business-bailout.

11. Ingraham, Christopher. "Wealth Concentration Returning to 'Levels Last Seen During the Roaring Twenties,' According to New Research," *Washington Post*, February 8, 2019. https://www.washingtonpost.com /us-policy/2019/02/08/wealth-concentration-returning-levels-Last -seen-during-roaring-twenties-according-new-research/.

12. "Changes in U.S. Family Finances from 2013 to 2016: Evidence from the Survey of Consumer Finances." Federal Reserve, September 2017. https://www.federalreserve.gov/publications/files/scf17.pdf.

13. "Poverty Thresholds." U.S. Census Bureau, last accessed September 3, 2020. https://www.census.gov/data/tables/time-series/demo/income -poverty/historical-poverty-thresholds.html.

14. Langston, Abbie, "100 Million and Counting: A Portrait of Economic Insecurity in the United States," PolicyLink, December 2018. https://www .policylink.org/resources-tools/100-million.

15. Richardson, Thomas, Peter Elliott, and Ronald Roberts. "The Relationship Between Personal Unsecured Debt and Mental and Physical Health: A Systematic Review and Meta-Analysis." *Clinical Psychology Review* 2, no. 8 (2013): 1148–62. https://pubmed.ncbi.nlm.nih.gov/24121465/.

16. Argys, Laura M., Andrew I. Friedson, and M. Melinda Pitts. "Killer Debt: The Impact of Debt on Mortality." Federal Reserve Bank of At-

lanta, November 2016. https://www.frbatlanta.org/-/media/documents /research/publications/wp/2016/14-killer-debt-the-impact-of-debt-on -mortality-2017-04-10.pdf.

17. Evans, Gary W. et al. "Childhood Poverty and Blood Pressure Reactivity to and Recovery from an Acute Stressor in Late Adolescence: The Mediating Role of Family Conflict." *Psychosomatic Medicine* 75, no. 7 (2013): 691–700. https://www.ncbi.nlm.nih.gov/pmc/articles/PMC3769521/.

18. Mitnik, Pablo A. "Economic Mobility in the United States." Pew Charitable Trusts, July 2015. https://www.pewtrusts.org/-/media/assets/2015 /07/fsm-irs-report_artfinal.pdf.

19. Isaacs, Julia B. "International Comparisons of Economic Mobility." Pew Charitable Trusts. https://www.brookings.edu/wp-content/uploads /2016/07/02_economic_mobility_sawhill_ch3.pdf. See also Jones, Katie. "Ranked: The Social Mobility of 82 Countries." Visual Capitalist, February 7, 2020. https://www.visualcapitalist.com/ranked-the-social-mobility -of-82-countries/.

20. Kiersz, Andy. "31 Countries Where the 'American Dream' Is More Attainable Than in the US," *Business Insider*, August 19, 2019. https://www .businessinsider.com.au/countries-where-intergenerational-mobility -american-dream-better-than-the-us-2019-8.

21. "The World Fact Book." Central Intelligence Agency, last accessed September 3, 2020. https://www.cia.gov/library/publications/the-world -factbook/rankorder/2102rank.html.

22. "Countries and Territories." Freedom House, last accessed September 3, 2020. https://freedomhouse.org/countries/freedom-world/scores?sort= desc&order=Total%20Score%20and%20Status.

23. Helliwell, John F. et al. "Social Environments for World Happiness." *World Happiness Report*. Sustainable Development Solutions Network, March 20, 2020. https://worldhappiness.report/ed/2020/social-environ ments-for-world-happiness/.

24. Henderson, Nia-Malika. "White Men Are 31 Percent of the American Population. They Hold 65 Percent of All Elected Offices," *Washington Post*, October 8, 2014. https://www.washingtonpost.com/news/the-fix /wp/2014/10/08/65-percent-of-all-american-elected-officials-are -white-men/.

25. Horowitz, Juliana Menasce, Ruth Igielnik, and Rakesh Kochhar. "Most Americans Say There Is Too Much Economic Inequality in the U.S., but Fewer Than Half Call It a Top Priority." Pew Research Center, January 9, 2020. https://www.pewsocialtrends.org/2020/01/09/most-americans-say -there-is-too-much-economic-inequality-in-the-u-s-but-fewer -than-half-call-it-a-top-priority/.

26. Abad-Santos, Alex. "Watch John Oliver Completely Destroy the Idea That Hard Work Will Make You Rich." *Vox*, July 14, 2014. https://www.vox.com/2014/7/14/5897797/john-oliver-explains-wealth-gap.

27. "Food Insecurity," Child Trends, September 28, 2018. https://www.childtrends.org/indicators/food-insecurity.

28. Lewis, Michael. "Extreme Wealth Is Bad for Everyone—Especially the Wealthy," *New Republic*, November 12, 2014. https://newrepublic.com/article/120092/billionaires-book-review-money-cant-buy-happiness.

29. Buchanan, Leigh. "American Entrepreneurship Is Actually Vanishing. Here's Why," *Inc.*, May 2015. https://www.inc.com/magazine/201505/leigh-buchanan/the-vanishing-startups-in-decline.html.

30. Eidelson, Josh and Luke Kawa. "Firing of Amazon Strike Leader Draws State and City Scrutiny," *Bloomberg*, March 30, 2020. https://www.bloomberg.com/news/articles/2020-03-30/amazon-worker-who-led-strike-over-virus-says-company-fired-him.

31. Hepler, Lauren. "Uber, Lyft and Why California's War Over Gig Work Is Just Beginning," Cal Matters, August 13, 2020. https://calmatters.org/economy/2020/08/california-gig-work-ab5-prop-22/.

32. Feiner, Lauren. "Uber CEO Says Its Service Will Probably Shut Down Temporarily in California If It's Forced to Classify Drivers As Employees," CNBC, August 12, 2020. https://www.cnbc.com/2020/08/12/uber-may-shut-down-temporarily-in-california.html.

33. Ingram, David. "Designed to Distract: Stock App Robinhood Nudges Users to Take Risks," NBC News, September 12, 2019. https://www.nbcnews.com/tech/tech-news/confetti-push-notifications-stock-app-robinhood-nudges-investors-toward-risk-n1053071. See also Shankar, Neil (@tallneil). "I just wanna live inside the world of these @Robinhood App illustrations." Twitter post, May 18, 2020. https://twitter.com/tallneil/status/1262401096577961984. And last, Knipfer, Matthew Q. "Optimally Climbing the Robinhood Cash Management Waitlist," Medium, November 5, 2019. https://medium.com/@MatthewQKnipfer/optimally-climbing-the-robinhood-cash-management-waitlist-f94218764ea7.

34. Geiger, A. W. and Leslie Davis. "A Growing Number of American Teenagers—Particularly Girls—Are Facing Depression." Pew Research Center, July 12, 2019. https://www.pewresearch.org/fact-tank/2019/07/12/a-growing-number-of-american-teenagers-particularly-girls-are-facing-depression/.

35. Shrikanth, Siddarth. "'Gamified' Investing Leaves Millennials Playing with Fire." *Financial Times*, May 6, 2020. https://www.ft.com/content/9336fd0f-2bf4-4842-995d-0bcbab27d97a.

36. Abbott, Briana. "Youth Suicide Rate Increased 56% in Decade, CDC Says," *Wall Street Journal*, October 17, 2019. https://www.wsj.com/arti cles/youth-suicide-rate-rises-56-in-decade-cdc-says-11571284861.

37. Mercado, Melissa C. et al. "Trends in Emergency Department Visits for Nonfatal Self-Inflicted Injuries Among Youth Aged 10 to 24 Years in the United States, 2001–2015." *Journal of the American Medical Association* 318, no. 19 (2017):1931–33. https://jamanetwork.com/journals/jama/full article/2664031.

38. Garcia-Navarro, Lulu. "The Risk of Teen Depression and Suicide Is Linked to Smartphone Use, Study Says," NPR, December 17, 2017. https://www.npr.org/2017/12/17/571443683/the-call-in-teens-and -depression.

39. Harris, Sam. "205: The Failure of Meritocracy: A Conversation with Daniel Markovits." *Making Sense* (podcast), May 22, 2020, 00:58:58. https://samharris.org/podcasts/205-failure-meritocracy/ (extended ep- isode version available through site membership).

40. Griffith, Erin and Kate Conger. "Palantir, Tech's Next Big I.P.O., Lost $580 Million in 2019," *New York Times*, August 21, 2020. https://www .nytimes.com/2020/08/21/technology/palantir-ipo-580-million-loss .html.

41. "Federal Receipt and Outlay Summary." Tax Policy Center. https:// www.taxpolicycenter.org/statistics/federal-receipt-and-outlay -summary.

42. Galloway, Scott. "A Post-Corona World." *Prof G Show* (podcast), March 26, 2020, 00:51:49. https://podcasts.apple.com/us/podcast/a -post-corona-world/id1498802610?i=1000469586627.

43. McKeever, Vicky. "Germany's Economic Response to the Coronavirus Crisis Is an Example for the World, Union Chief Says," CNBC, May 1, 2020. https://www.cnbc.com/2020/05/01/coronavirus-germany-ilo-chief -says-it-set-a-global-economic-example.html.

44. Goodman, Peter S., Patricia Cohen, and Rachel Chaundler. "European Workers Draw Paychecks. American Workers Scrounge for Food," *New York Times*, July 3, 2020. https://www.nytimes.com/2020/07/03/busi ness/economy/europe-us-jobless-coronavirus.html.

45. "Flattening the Curve on COVID-19," UNDP, April 16, 2020. http:// www.undp.org/content/seoul_policy_center/en/home/presscenter/ar ticles/2019/flattening-the-curve-on-covid-19.html.

46. Divine, John. "Does Congress Have an Insider Trading Problem?" *US News*, August 6, 2020. https://money.usnews.com/investing/stock -market-news/articles/does-congress-have-an-insider-trading -problem. Bainbridge, Stephen. "Insider Trading Inside the Beltway"

(2010). https://www.researchgate.net/publication/228231180_Insider
_Trading_Inside_the_Beltway.

47. "War Production," PBS, last accessed September 3, 2020. https://www
.pbs.org/thewar/at_home_war_production.htm. See also "The Auto Industry Goes to War," Teaching History. https://teachinghistory.org/his
tory-content/ask-a-historian/24088.

48. Davis, Wade. "The Unraveling of America," *Rolling Stone*, August 6, 2020.
https://www.rollingstone.com/politics/political-commentary/covid-19
-end-of-american-era-wade-davis-1038206/.

49. Flamm, Bradley. "Putting the Brakes on 'Non-Essential' Travel: 1940s
Wartime Mobility, Prosperity, and the US Office of Defense." *The Journal of Transport History* 27. no. 1 (2006): 71–92. https://www.research
gate.net/publication/233547720_Putting_the_brakes_on_%27nones
sential%27_travel_1940s_wartime_mobility_prosperity_and_the_US
_Office_of_Defense. "Draft Resistance and Evasion." Encylopedia.com,
last accessed September 3, 2020. https://www.encyclopedia.com/his
tory/encyclopedias-almanacs-transcripts-and-maps/draft-resistance
-and-evasion.

# ABOUT THE AUTHOR

**Scott Galloway** is Professor of Marketing at NYU's Stern School of Business and a serial entrepreneur. In 2012, he was named one of the world's best business professors by Poets & Quants. He has founded nine companies, including Prophet, Red Envelope, and L2. He is the bestselling author of *The Four* and *The Algebra of Happiness* and has served on the boards of directors of The New York Times Company, Urban Outfitters, and UC Berkeley's Haas School of Business. His *Prof G* and *Pivot* podcasts, *No Mercy / No Malice* blog, and Prof G YouTube channel reach millions. In 2020, *Adweek* named *Pivot* Business Podcast of the Year. In 2019, Scott founded Section4, an online education platform for working professionals where he teaches business strategy: section4.com.